Mingled Voices 4

International Proverse Poetry Prize Anthology 2019

Proverse Hong Kong

2020

MINGLED VOICES 4 is an anthology of one hundred and twenty-four poems, the work of sixty-nine poets, selected from those which were entered in the fourth annual international competition for the International Proverse Poetry Prize in 2019.

The International Proverse Poetry Prize was jointly founded in 2016 by Dr Gillian Bickley and Dr Verner Bickley MBE, in association with the annual international Proverse Prize for unpublished book-length fiction, non-fiction or poetry, submitted in English, which they also founded, in 2008.

Poems could be submitted on any subject or topic, chosen by each poet, or on the subject chosen for 2019 by the Administrators, "Plastic" (interpreted in any way each writer chose). There was a free choice of interpretation, form and style.

Included in the anthology are the poems that won the first, second, and third prizes. Selection to appear in the anthology was also awarded as a prize by the judges for the Prize. This year, special mention is additionally made of six of these poets.

MINGLED VOICES 4
INTERNATIONAL PROVERSE POETRY PRIZE ANTHOLOGY
2019

Poets

Abbie Taylor, Ahmed Elbeshlawy, Aiden Heung,
Allegra Jostad Silberstein, Andy Peyrie, Angelo Rizzi,
Anne Casey, Annie Christain, Anson Wang,
Aparna Upadhyaya Sanyal, Brittany Mishra,
Bruce Arlen Wasserman, C.N. Rajalakshmi, C.W. Emerson,
Carol Flake Chapman, Carrie Hooper, Dah Helmer,
Deepa Vanjani, Edward Tiesse,
Fiona Chen, George Watt, Halil Suat Saraç,
Harsh Ramchandani, Hayley Ann Solomon, Helen Davis,
Helen Oliver, Ian Chambers, Iris Litt,
Jennifer Ann Eagleton, Joanna Radwańska-Williams,
Joy Al-Sofi, Jun Pan, Kate Hawkins, Keith Nunes,
Lawdenmarc Decamora, Liam Blackford, Libby Wong,
Luisa Ternau, Lynda Lambert, Maggie Wong,
Maria Elena Blanco, Marjory Woodfield,
Martin Jon Porter, Matthew Harris, M. Ann Reed,
Mocco Wollert, Neil Douglas, Paola Caronni,
Patience O'Neill, Patrick Reardon, Peter Verbica,
Raymond Calbay, Rayn Epremian,
Reema Baniabbasi, Rena Ong,
R.J. Keeler, Rony Nair, Simona Rackova,
Solomon Au Yeung, Stéphane D'Amour,
Sui Ping Au Yeung, Susan Lavender, Suzanne Cottrell,
Teresa Ngan-fung Chu, Thea Biesheuvel,
Vincent Casaregola, Vinni Relwani,
Wayne Mattingly, Zachary Knox

Editors

Gillian Bickley · Verner Bickley

Proverse Hong Kong

Mingled Voices 4
International Proverse Poetry Prize Anthology 2019
edited by Gillian Bickley and Verner Bickley.
First published in paperback in Hong Kong
by Proverse Hong Kong, 21 April 2020.
Copyright © Proverse Hong Kong 2020.
Each author retains the copyright in the poem(s)
that appear over his/her own name.
ISBN: 978-988-8491-89-6

Enquiries to:
Proverse Hong Kong, P.O. Box 259, Tung Chung Post Office,
Tung Chung, Lantau Island, NT, Hong Kong SAR, China.
E-mail: proverse@netvigator.com;
Web: www.proversepublishing.com

Page design by Proverse Hong Kong.
Cover design by Pin-Key Design Co.

British Library Cataloguing in Publication Data.
A catalogue record for this book is available
from the British Library.

Mingled Voices 4: Proverse Poetry Prize Anthology 2019

MESSAGE FROM THEA BIESHEUVEL
Second-prize winner
International Proverse Poetry Prize (2018)

Writers are by nature solitary people. Our relationship is between our thoughts and the page or the screen, using a variety of aids such as pens or fingers on keyboards.

Competitors, on the other hand, need others in order to see who is better at "it". To compete means to pit your skills against someone else's.

The two aspects, thoughts and super effort, seem at opposite ends of the spectrum. Sometimes you just know that you've written something that not only feels good to you, but when you read it out, or give the page to someone else, it evokes the same feelings in them as you had when you wrote it. That's what we are all looking for, isn't it? It is certainly what brings me to the point of seeing where else I can send my poem; who else might read it and feel the same?

As I get older I appreciate more and more what might have motivated my mother and father to do what they did. They packed us all up and moved us across the world. Not a land that we'd heard of or enticed us. Somewhere far away from the war and strife around us.

And yet, having abandoned all they knew, their memories were of "home". Their reflections were not often shared with us as children, but as we got older. My reflections of my mother moved from incomprehension, to anger and finally, to a sympathy for that woman she had become. It was therefore very private. I shared it with some students in my class which resulted in tears from some.

Original settlers in my adopted country don't show much sympathy for those who've come across the seas to join them. I knew the poem had to have an International audience.

The Proverse competition fitted like a glove.

I've since sent off other poems in various directions and don't really expect to hear again. That's life when you're a solitary writer.

To get acknowledged for my contribution so promptly and positively was (and still is) too positive to file away. To meet with the organisers and other competitors was a bonus contributed by my husband.

Talking to other poets about their work makes writing poetry seem as normal as breathing, not something esoteric and quaint. It affirms the inner life of us poets.

Getting a prize for my work was certainly the icing on the cake.

I'll be submitting some other work, of course!

Thea Biesheuvel
Brisbane, Australia
January 2020

ACKNOWLEDGEMENTS

All those at Proverse Hong Kong, administrators of the Proverse Poetry Prize (single poems), thank all those who entered for the 2019 competition, and warmly appreciate the helpful and willing participation in the editorial process of those whose poems were selected for this anthology.

We are most grateful, also, for the professionalism and dedication of the judges.

The Hotel Coma, Ordino, Principat d'Andorra, is warmly thanked for their willing, friendly, and ongoing help with practicalities.

NOTE FROM THE EDITORS
and Proverse Poetry Prize Administrators

For this, the fourth annual international Proverse Poetry Prize, poems were invited, either on the entrant's own choice of subject or theme, or on a subject selected by the Proverse Poetry Prize Administrators, "Plastic" (interpreted as each entrant might wish). Any form, style or genre could be used.

Poems were judged by the panel of judges as submitted and the following awards were made:

First Prize
Maria Elena Blanco, 'Waiting for Ulysses'
Second Prize
Aiden Heung, 'A Stranger on the Street'
Third Prizes
Vincent Casaregola, 'The Plastic Dead'
Anne Casey, 'Either way, the fact remains'
Carol Flake Chapman, 'Under the Blue Tarps'
Brittany Mishra, 'And Then Eve'

Special mention
Ian Chambers, M. Ann Reed, Deepa Vanjani,
Peter Verbica, George Watt, Marjorie Woodfield.

Several other entered poems were awarded a place in this
International Proverse Poetry Prize Anthology 2019,
Mingled Voices 4.
Their names appear in the Table of Contents
as well as on the title page.

Congratulations to all!

Several of the poems in the Anthology were edited by the writers after selection for the Anthology and before publication, but no further judging of the entries was made at this stage.

All writers were invited to contribute a commentary or notes on their poems for this anthology and have responded in different ways.

Brief biographies of those whose work is represented in *Mingled Voices 4* are included in the anthology.

To the extent that those whose poetry is published here tell us about their occupations and/or working lives, we know that among them are authors and writers (including of ESL materials, fantasy novels, legal texts, musicals, non-fiction, science fiction, screenplays, TV scripts), editors, essayists, journalists (including a part-time columnist), literary critics, playwrights, poets, researchers, translators (including of Italian, Spanish, and poetry), a media communications director, a former academic librarian, teachers and retired teachers at different levels and for different groups (including of those with dyslexia) and in different areas (including American literature and film, art history, English, composition, creative writing, discourse analysis, English Literature, ESL, Fine Arts, Humanities, interpreting, Italian and German languages, rhetorical studies, Slavic and English Linguistics, studio art, stylistics, Theory of Knowledge, translating, voice and piano), a clinical psychologist, a doctor in general practice, actors, a voice-over artist, television presenters, radio broadcasters, a photographer, a filmmaker, lawyers and former lawyers, a musician, an occasional blacksmith, a potter, an engineer, an aeronautical engineer.

Again, to the extent that those who hold degrees make explicit mention of them (and not all do), we know that among them they hold degrees (including at Bachelor's and Master's levels) in astrophysics, Computer Science, Computer Systems Management, counseling psychology and psychology, creative writing, Czech Language and Literature, English and Linguistics, English Language and Literature, English Literature, Fine Arts, French, German and vocal performance, International Relations, interpreting studies, Law, literature, literature and communication, Spanish and Latin American literatures, Mathematics, music performance, Librarianship, Linguistics, Media Arts. One has a Certificate in Poetry. It is clear that among them are also several who hold PhDs. A few are still undergoing their initial formal education.

One is an Honorman, U.S. Naval Submarine School. "SS" (Submarine Service) qualified. Vietnam Service Medal. Honorable Discharge.

Poems were submitted from Australia, Austria, Canada, the Czech Republic, France, Hong Kong, India, Ireland, Italy, Macau, New Zealand, the Philippines, Singapore, Turkey, the Peoples' Republic of China, the United Kingdom, the United Arab Emirates and the United States of America.

The countries of birth of these poets include Australia, Cuba, the Czech Republic, Egypt, Germany, Hong Kong, India, Ireland, Italy, New Zealand, Poland, South Africa, the Netherlands, South Africa, the Peoples' Republic of China, the Philippines, the United Arab Emirates, the United Kingdom, the United States of America, Turkey.

Some are new or young writers. Others are already well-published as poets, whether in magazines and journals or in book form; some with several published poetry collections of their own. Some are prize-winning writers and/or winners of grants to support their literary work. Several have participated in national and international poetry festivals and other prestigious events. Some are leaders in that they have formed poetry writing and/or appreciation groups, including online writing communities. Others have influential positions in the publishing world. For at least twenty-one of the sixty-nine, English is not their mother-tongue.

*

Entrants were asked to submit their work in English. To qualify, entries needed to be previously unpublished in English, but could have been previously published in another language.

Poems were invited in any genre, form, or style. Nearly all are in free verse; some use idiosyncratic patternings; and a small number use specific forms like the haiban, haiku and quasi-haiku, and acrostic. One adopts a Chinese poetic form. One is in what we might call poetic prose. Poetic techniques such as repetition, alliteration, lists, contrasts, chorus are used. There is one delightful pun on the name of the English seaside town, "Morecombe". There is ebullient vocabulary, sophisticated and masterly use of the run-on line. Some are allusive and symbolist. There are echoes from a biblical and classical education. Perhaps most are written in the voice of the writer but some present a persona, speaking in the form of a dramatic monologue. (The "back-stories" provided for many of the poems help us to know which are which.)

A wide range of subjects, situations, events, arguments, moods and emotions is displayed in the anthology as a whole. Most writers chose to enter a poem on a subject or theme of their own choice although the subject selected by the Proverse Poetry Prize Administrators—"Plastic" (interpreted as each writer might desire)—proved to be relatively popular, with about thirty per cent of the total number of poems being inspired by this topic, including the four third-prize winners. Broadly speaking, some of the thirty per cent spoke of plastic in a negative way—some leaning towards the topic set for 2016, "the Environment"—but some saw the positive qualities of plastic; others focused on or referred to the qualities of plasticity and flexibility. A few combined different aspects and uses of plastic and plasticity in a single poem. Poems on self-chosen topics spoke of the family, rural and urban landscapes, personal experiences and epiphanies, political and geopolitical events and crimes.

Each poem was judged on its own merits and those selected for this anthology are arranged simply in alphabetical order of poets' surnames and (where more than one poem by a single poet is included) also by title (unless a different sequence was requested by a poet). The poets' commentaries and notes on their poems, requested during the editing process, are presented as endnotes. The brief biographies of the poets (which were not known to the judges at the time of judging) appear in alphabetical order of poets' surnames.

THE INTERNATIONAL
PROVERSE POETRY PRIZE 2020

We very much hope that all who entered for the Proverse Poetry Prize 2019 and all who were awarded a place in *Mingled Voices 4, the Proverse Poetry Prize Anthology 2019* will continue to enter their work in future years. We continue to welcome all those who entered for the Prize in 2016, 2017, and 2018 and all who were awarded a place in previous International Proverse Poetry Prize Anthologies, *Mingled Voices, Mingled Voices 2* and *Mingled Voices 3*. It is a pleasure to recognize as repeat entrants the names of those who have entered before and to compare and contrast their current entry or entries with what we have seen before. We are also always pleased to see new names and we hope that there will be more new entrants in 2020 and beyond.

Receipt of entries for the 2020 competition begins on 7 May 2020 with 30 June 2020 as the deadline.

As in previous years, poets may enter poems either on a subject or theme of their own choice or on the theme suggested by the Administrators for 2020, 'Hunger', interpreted as each poet may wish. Full and updated details will usually be available on the Proverse website, proversepublishing.com.

In the meantime, we hope that those whose poems are included in the 2019 International Proverse Poetry Prize Anthology will enjoy seeing their and others' work and that all their readers will share the pleasure of the judges and the editors in these "Mingled Voices".

Gillian Bickley and Verner Bickley
Hong Kong

PREFACE

A competition which allows entrants to submit, if they so desire, just one poem is a reminder that it is not unusual to be remembered for one poem. When my husband and I bought our home in the Cotswolds many years ago, our surveyor's name happened to be Dowson. By way of an introductory chat we asked if he was in any way related to the poet Ernest Dowson. In some astonishment he replied that he was, adding that Dowson was remembered now for one poem. At this point we quoted in unison "I have been faithful to thee, Cynara, in my fashion". Perhaps that was a good omen for the writers featured in *Mingled Voices 4*.

The title of Maria Blanco's poem, 'Waiting for Ulysses', touches on the traditional and universally accepted story of the return of the hero Ulysses from the Trojan war. Legend relates that, after many years of wanderings, many delays and dangers on his return journey, he arrived home to find his wife Penelope waiting patiently. The reader soon discovers that there is another narrative here. The lines:

> Waiting for Ulysses I am not
> Waiting for Ulysses
> He is coming to me

present a very different interpretation of the situation, and one that will change the accepted view and prove uncomfortable for the returned hero. Instead of the patient wife fending off unwanted suitors, we find Penelope in the mode of stern interrogator and judge, requiring her husband to give an account of his sojourn with dangerous and alluring sirens, Circe, Nausicaa and Calypso. The playful literary associations with other well-known authors like Joyce and Beckett suggested by the "Waiting" of her title prepare us for the grim humour when Ulysses is also required to give an account not only of his conduct but of his "valuables" too.

In his poem, 'A Stranger on the Street', Aidan Heung reflects on the disquiet we feel at the sight of homeless people on our streets. He examines the tensions between two opposing views which for him seem to spring from two quite distinct philosophies of life: on the one hand is the ancient Confucian way of the Analects which prescribes kindness to the unfortunates in life, and on the other hand is the practical economic view which finds them a hindrance and a burden on our economy. His metaphor of the juggernaut of History is aptly chosen to present the fate of those who cannot escape being crushed under its wheels. Again Heung, without being in the least didactic, draws on the more spiritual attitude in likening the man living on the street to the "bodhisattva" the passer-by is "afraid to look at". There is certainly an element of , "There but for the grace of God go I", in his poem.

The winners of the third prize challenge the reader with interesting views also.

Anne Casey's poem, 'Either way, the Fact Remains', reflects the ambivalence at the heart of the "fact" of climate change: all the statements that people make on the subject can be turned upside down – a timely reminder to the fanatics on both sides, that they do not know the whole story. Her centrally placed word, "That", given a line to itself, forms the pivot on which the arguments of both sides can be turned and balanced.

The suggested theme of, "Plastic", prompted a variety of responses. Brittany Mishra's , 'And then Eve', has some telling images of the creation and destiny of woman.

Her creator:

smoothed her curves,
and 3D printed her heart out of hard, breakable plastic.

She can smell the apple of temptation but is doomed to be forever blamed for the expulsion from the garden of Eden and subject to the authority of men.

Carol Flake Chapman's, 'Under the Blue Tarps', notes the steady rise in the number of sightings of the plastic tarpaulin sheets used as temporary cover after the natural or man-made disasters of fire, earthquake, flood and warfare. They are now ubiquitous, flapping their presence in every continent. Their worldwide presence registers our unease:

As we lose the sense of safety we thought we held
As the waters keep rising and the winds keep blowing.

In his poem, 'The Plastic Dead', Vincent Casaregola recalls the plastic toy soldiers he played with as a boy. Among the figures, suggesting with their guns, grenades and knives the heroics of war, his memory lingers on the casualties of war tucked away in each cardboard box. Their plastic forms betray none of the signs of their violent end:

> they lay grim but peaceful, unmutilated
> but for the vagaries of chance

Some poets impress by conveying deep feeling in tightly controlled verse that avoids sentimentality or nostalgia, as does Ian Chambers in, 'The Dying of the Light', where one phone call confirms the breaking of the intimate bond between the child and the mother who bore him many years ago

> when I lay, as now, wombed
> In darkness, my heartbeat
> Driven by yours.

Chambers also conveys in, 'Donegal', the strong sense of being rooted in the landscape of the country which was home to him and his ancestors.

Ann Reed's, 'Sighting Polaris', is a hymn to the power of beauty in nature, in music, in architecture to soften the pain of the sick and the bereaved.

Deepa Vanjani's, 'The Mask-Maker's Bian Lian', confirms that a mask of a human face, informed with 'Love and bliss, wisdom and knowledge', can transform the despot who adopts it into a compassionate human being.

Peter Verbica's poem, 'From the Scent of Trees', records the unpopularity of prophets and the tedium they generate in ordinary mortals; but even his chosen exemplar Enoch can be distracted by the scents of the earth.

As he gazes on the flow of a river in Zhejiang Province, George Watt watches the stream of, "polyclonal, polydipsic, polystyrene", foam sweeping by on its way to the ocean. But in, 'Desire in Winter: in memoriam', he likens himself to a, "sad, phony Orpheus", listening for the sounds of spring

somewhere in a vast lucent cavern,
crystal strung.

 But the cold uncomfortable world breaks in and his desire
thaws into the desire for a warm bath and a fresh face.

Marjorie Woodfield's poem 'She visits from New
Zealand' reflects on the unappealing aspects of the modern
where the, "crisp new housing blocks", are unloved by their
inhabitants. The older generation, brought here from their old
homes, remember being surrounded by the ancient splendours
of Arabia where the Aramaic letters of the sculptors, dating
from 31 AD, can still be traced.

Look beyond the prize winners and find many poems which
appeal on a number of levels.

For example, Neil Douglas in his poem, 'Nan Lian
Garden', treats with wry humour our concern to hold in check
the human tendency to despoil with our carelessness the
beauty we travel so far to see: what a contrast between some
natural feature or great architecture, the "Truth in beauty", and
the regulations imposed on our viewing!

Joanna Radwanska-Williams, in her poem, 'The Pendant',
knows the conflicting emotions roused by a beautiful jewel:

carved oval
set with diamonds.

The craftsman's gem is a calcified coral: we are seduced by its
beauty while knowing that it is, "A tear of blood".

Liam Blackford's, 'Untitled 1', presents a timely reminder
that our cherished views on issues of the day are not, as we like
to feel, original: they are filtered through a complexity of

corporate memory,
bestseller consciousness,
standard forms, tribal rites.

He also knows that in human affairs, "noise carries the
furthest."

In her poem, 'The Butterfly Effect', Hayley Ann Solomon rejoices in the sweetness and shimmer of the butterflies' wings while being aware that in our inter-connected world the:

> Wrappings, laminates, careless bags and straws
> Are the flapping wings of butterfly,
> In the universe of laws

In an allusion to a phrase from Scripture she makes the appeal:

> We knew not what we did.

Plastic is occasionally allowed to answer back. Maggie Wong permits plastic to remind human beings of its sensational rise to power over a century since its birth. In its own defence, it points out the hypocrisy in enjoying its benefits while not uniting to fight that ascendancy.—"Bah! Humbug!"—Indeed.

Meanwhile, Libby Wong allows plastic to boast its uses to the world:

> I'm versatile, malleable, pliable and synthetic,
> Studied at the university and polytechnic.

The reader will find more than one poem that resonates and challenges here.

Margaret Clarke
Translator of *Le Monde tel qu'il sera* (1846)
by Émile Souvestre and co-translator with her husband,
the author I.F.Clarke, of *Le Dernier Homme* (1805)
by Jean-Baptiste François Xavier Cousin De Grainville
Oxfordshire, UK

CONTENTS

POEMS

POEMS

Alive[1]

You just don't know
what it means to be alive
till you see yourself reflected
in the eyes
of a Nile crocodile.

Glittering,
green
you
in an agate eye
watching you
watching it.

Look into the eyes
of a Nile crocodile
knowing what it means
to be alive.

Joy Al-Sofi

Holiday![2]

Hong Kongers take great holidays.—
I've, myself, taken quite a few.
Airfare takes you anywhere
And brings you back home too.

Picture yourself: in Paris
A coffee on the Champs;
Strudel in Vienna;
Foliage in Vermont.

More than enough to choose from—
Any one of them will do:
Architecture, culture, historic relics too.
A nod to Mother Nature?—
Grand Canyon's got the view.

Spanish Steps and minarets,
Buddhist temples, Shinto shrines,
Riverboats and mountain slopes,
Sistine Chapel, Windsor Castle,
New York nightlife, Kenyan wildlife,
Michelin dining,
Great Wall walks.

Every four minutes
From Chek Lap Kok,
They'll take you and bring you back.

When you go
You just don't know
Who is coming back:
You,
The same, or
You,

Forever changed.

Joy Al-Sofi

A Paged Bag

To peel the midnight skin in a sharp myth,
the same dust dancing in flames, hanging in air before the
same old mirror;
And to swallow in mines, the bloods glued all over my
teething cranes;

one steamy scoop after another,
such was the confessing crunch of hullabaloos,
to be once shared, and then secretly prayed for, us dressed as
     gurus?

Praying for such selves,
well-carved only on those fertile days,
the much yellowed chronicles;
now arranged in our old myopic gaze...

until one bite, Again, clinging through those pages,
coming back to that uncontaminated lapse,
to unlock that same tiring soul,
& to wait for those dated childhood tags,

labelling a seed that so wanted to fit in,
but was held back from its very nature of no return:
soon to be Chopped, Scrambled, and Sold, in some
unknown urn...

Solomon Au Yeung

Sailing[3]

On the shore, imagine there's light
on the other side, never turns on
only the fragments of waves and stinging sea

maybe the sea a mirage, letting those ships go into
nothingness
and daytime without white flowers
a yellow raincoat scattered in the sky
white flowers were in blossom overnight, covering
wastelands
arrived in endless pier with non-stop swinging

lie at illusion
convoyed by nothingness

a lifebuoy saves some spray of yesterday
another row of spray comes back
following thousands of anonymous waves
inherits the house of the house of phantoms
in a watery kingdom

Sui Ping Au Yeung

Plastic Violence[4]

I never knew how something so flimsy smooth
could have such sharp edges.
I see it in their eyes;
see-through but can't get through
even with a piercing smile or a bursting chuckle
or with the claws of a big bear hug.

Their sharp presence a cling-wrap air
we breathe in bits and gulps,
schooled into fish and sea turtles munching
on that late trend no longer the latest,
on those toys we thought we outgrew,
on those bottles carrying secrets
we thought we neatly stacked and recycled
or incinerated away,
on those bags; flags fanning a rush
of collective emotional eating.

Is this the cost of clinging
so tightly against delicate drops
seeping through?

*Handwritten with a plastic pen in a Moleskine stripped from
its plastic wrapping.*

Reema Baniabbasi

<h1 style="text-align:center">Sempiternity[5]</h1>

Houses surrender to time
wilderness gardens
time past equals time remaining
telling stories
coloured memories
rusted car bodies frame a creek
dead leaves like dandruff
ducks dive for muddy morsels
dragonflies meditating
currawongs sing Vivaldi.
A double edged landscape of endurance.

Winds rush to nowhere
long grass seethes at their impudence
and bends at the last
shows forbearance
night windows blink like campfires
light the way
glow-worms in a cave of time
remain vigilant
defy the dark
country sings its dreamtime.
A double-edged history of culture.

Thea Biesheuvel

Sermon on the Mound (of garbage)[6]

There once were oceans of calm delight
where fish and people played.
The sparkling, caressing light
chased dark thoughts, caused pains to fade.

Blessed be the pure.

And many rivers ran a rocky course
precarious cliffs cascaded
climbed by both men and horse
to go where people traded.

Blessed be the industrious.

By the Biblical rivers of Babylon
plastic bottles, cartons, strands of nylon.
A growing mound of rotting refuse
rusting ammunition, guns out of use.

Blessed be those who lived in Zion.

On the Yellow river, Yangtze
oily ribbons weave a Fancy*
no lessons from the Monkey King
just slimy, putrid logs contaminating everything.

Curses to oil-coloured excrement.

The Mighty Mekong is all wrong
transparent pieces, plastic so light
they look like jellyfish and pong*
Fools fish and fishermen alike.

Curses to killers of cormorants…

Many rivers still run their rocky courses
where polymers persist.
There is no denying we have caused this hurt.
It's not the earth the meek inherit, it's the dirt.

Thea Biesheuvel

Untitled 1[7]

Core hub influencers,
key opinion leaders,
copycats, dilettantes,
tastemakers, outsiders,
hacks, mavericks, casuals,
stans, posers, purists, fakes.

No ideas are new.
The past shapes all action.
Our thoughts come off the rack:
corporate memory,
bestseller consciousness,
standard forms, tribal rites.

A meme is a virus:
it is passed through contact
with speech, sound and writing.
Language is the channel;
culture is the symptom.
We are all carriers.

The mind is a raindish,
exposed to the heavens,
spilling over with rain,
oil, sand, heavy metals,
bacteria, acids,
and reactive compounds.

All social upheaval
has systemic causes:
accretion of stresses;
unbalanced feedback loops;
unaddressed errors; and
high acceleration.

All legacy platforms
generate junk content
to smokescreen their failures.
When noise and clarity
compete for attention,
noise carries the farthest.

Liam Blackford

Untitled 2

All human processes
can receive a structure
to induce their meaning.
How can technology
assist us with this task,
and has it helped so far?

As cold begets the fire,
the truth begets the news;
the mass begets the niche.
In a world in action,
systems, in response to
conditions, so emerge.

Luxury generates
relaxation at points
and tension at others.
Thus, it is like the truth.
Potent but dangerous;
sought after but not grasped.

To whom much is given,
much is well expected.
For whom the spoils are great,
the taxes are greater.
At whom light shines on high,
a long shadow is cast.

Violence is the midwife
of new societies,
by which heterodox
becomes true orthodox,
right and first and chosen
for friends and foes alike.

In an advanced culture,
today's models of art,
media, politics,
leisure, entertainment,
and hospitality
would not need to apply.

Liam Blackford

Untitled 3[8]

Forum cum dialogue
on development of
basic infrastructure
in belt and road countries.
Our greatest minds share views
and circulate insights.

A new rail terminal
will link Hong Kong up with
44 new cities.
It is a great feat of
political, legal
and technical design.

信息公得同步。
人民所接触的
成为所接受的。
充分控制信息、
把噪音弄清澈
是领导的责任。

我国所有道路
都归回到首都。
这里藏着势力
抢得翻天覆地。
长期以来如此，
也会永远依旧。

Time is a spiral form.
It grows and advances
piercing a new way
but retaining a link
to a core origin
which is never broken.

When freedom is too great,
the people are exposed
to collateral harm.
When the pace is too fast,
they burn upon entry
to a violent future.

Liam Blackford

Waiting For Ulysses[9]

Waiting for Ulysses
is the title of a poem
is a way of pretending
is a manner of discourse
is not a matter of fact.
It is a wink at Beckett
a bow to Kavafis
a laugh with Joyce
hardly a real laugh.
We know how it all ends:
No Exit
Lost Illusions
Dangerous Relations.
It is all but literature
and it is all literature.
Thus we are done with
waiting for
waiting out
waiting on
waiting by
and just plain waiting.

Waiting for Ulysses I am not
waiting for Ulysses.
He is coming to me
and no (other) gods
are there to save him.
He has some business pending
here at Sirens' Reef
having to do with
cleansing his bad name
his bad manners
his bad breath
his bad karma.
Sly of mind he is,
haughty with language,
a tinge of red in his hands.

(He'd better deal with all that
thinks he reluctantly
lest he once more awaken
the wrath of Zeus).
Slightly distraught now
he hears voices.

I am Circe,
bent, stark naked, on catching the ideal husband.
I bring you fantasies
(sexually delirious, you revel
in my sultry night games).
I am Nausicaa,
secretly dreaming of the ideal husband
Chaste, I give you just a glance of me
(you are enticed, but move on
and keep your pleasure to yourself).
I am Calypso,
offering bed and board to the ideal husband
I charm you with my songs
(you buy our wedded bliss, later
get bored, long for Penelope).
I am Penelope,
waiting for the return of my ideal husband
I keep our vows
surrounded by my lovers
(distrustful, you come back in disguise).

I am Athena.
I say stop. And beware.
A new Iliad has started.
Paris was abducted by Helen.
You are expected here
at Sirens' Reef
at my behest.

I give you twenty minutes
to review your deeds of the last twenty years,
to repent for twenty-plus centuries
of your disastrous "man" kind,
to reset your genes and reprogramme
your values (and your valuables)
to reprocess your words
and speak to me
eye to eye
in the language of poetry.

Maria Elena Blanco

Nothing to declare[10]

I.

Is the exit we're headed to,
But the baggage carousel remains
Unflinching, imprudently stopping us
And fellow passengers on our tracks,
Holding hostage our checked-in bags
And whatever valuable enough to
Cross the skies and get labeled as
Priority, heavy, fragile and
Handle with care.

II.

The conveyor belt is still unmoving
At the one hour mark, and people start
Complaining about scheduled connecting flights,
While we could only curse in a language
No one here would anyway understand.
Is our aggravation worse than what's faced
By those waiting on the other side of arrival?

III.

We grab our luggage, heavier than expected,
But instead it tries to rein us in.
Regaining foothold, we push toward
The green lane of the contraband-free,
Pass the blank stare of the customs officer,
And follow signs to exit the airport.
Absent any itinerary, we finally go.

Raymond Calbay

Arboreal Witness[11]

Your long arms—
Reassuring, maternal,
stained with the white scales of time,
give me a second welcome
as the sky blushes
and covers the idle Irrawaddy with a pink film.
A boat spits out loud crackles
And marks with its passage
the end of daily tasks.

The banks are thirsty.
You, immutable and prosperous—
careful silent sentinel of an eternal valley,
where spare red bricks crumbled
with the grumbling of the earth's belly.
Pinnacles fell from the temples' roofs
like Buddhas' heads cut off and stolen—
or past heroes betrayed by men in uniform,
who sat down quietly to eat lahpet
under your weeping canopy.

Every now and then,
a bride shows up.
Her eyes, like mine, turn to your branches
with the wish to untangle the thoughts
you've captured from us.

The train of her white dress bears the fragrance
of something new and clean,
and takes in the dead leaves that you dropped
while blessing her footsteps.

Paola Caronni

Restless Night[12]

I wake up to the sound of wind—
slamming windows, banging doors.
The waves crash livid in the sea,
And the echo reverberates
like the words
of broken promises.

As the night slowly leaves the scene,
A gecko performs his song to his lover,
a bird refines his repetitions,
doves are cooing.

I listen, in silence,
and marvel at
the first sunrays
that sneak through the blinds of my room.

The curtain is moved by the wind,
like a flag on its mast.
Its shadows dance on the wall
and improvise puppets' stories.

I long for the chirping of cicadas.
that takes me
to a childhood spent in the fields
of my homeland,
somersaulting
and running down hills of thick grass
while chasing butterflies
with blushed cheeks and scratched knees.
Laughing.

It's been so long.
The world still revolves around beauty.
	As if it were all.

Paola Caronni

The Plastic Dead[13]

As a child, I collected small plastic
soldiers from the Second World War,
soldiers molded in olive green,
in twelve different poses—with rifles,
pistols, grenades, and even knives.
Some were lighter green, some darker,
to indicate two opposing sides,
different in their hearts or minds.

Then toymakers grew ambitious,
diversified to offer fighting men
in exact shapes and uniforms—
the Americans remained green,
while the British were light brown,
the Germans, of course, were grey,
and the Japanese, a sort of yellow tan.
For authenticity, several plastic dead
came hidden in each cardboard box,

small men of plastic who had died
in the imagined violence of imagined war,
but their bodies expressed no horrors—
they lay grim but peaceful, unmutilated
but for the vagaries of chance or
the malicious cunning of small boys.
I have long since lost track
of the many troops of toys.
No matter. I sometimes
dream of them, especially of
the plastic dead, arranged in neat rows,
    when I knew too little to bury them.

Vincent Casaregola

Either way, the fact remains[14]

There is no way back
Therefore we can no longer hold as irrefutable truth that
Every human heart has sufficient good at its core
That we could muster the collective will necessary to save
         our precious planet
There is no denying
We are capable of taking the measures necessary for our
own survival
To secure the future for us and the almost nine million
species around us
We could make the right choices
The fact remains that
Earth cannot repair itself
There is no basis even from advanced satellite findings to
show that
Earth and all who dwell on her can survive the impacts of
human activities
The greatest scientific minds of our time attest that
The world's largest living structure, the Great Barrier Reef,
is on-path to certain destruction
That
Over two thousand species from sea-level to two thousand
metres deep are destined to perish
We can no longer support the assertion that
There is always a way—
There is a way to undo the damage we have done—
Allowing that we make every effort to counter global
excesses
The impact of human activities is irreversible
Although we may think
That we can take action to fix this
We cannot deny the inevitability
That not one of us can make a difference
Nature cannot heal itself
We can no longer lie to ourselves that
This devastation can be reversed

(Now read each line from the bottom up.)
Anne Casey

Donegal[15]

I look across a rusty landscape shot with harsh
morning sun. Crisp leaves, curled and crinkled, the colour
of the breathing fields, are torn from decaying branches
by the wild Atlantic air, dancing and scattering

before coming to rest beneath mossy walls.
Trees huddle together along tortuous tracks,
wind at their backs, anchored in the hardy grasses
and heathers, hesitating, leaning like the old farmer

wending his way home after feeding his rams,
gnarled stick in a gnarled hand.
Here and there turf smoke, dragged from silent stone
chimneys, dissipates like winter breath and away

to the south I can see the scars of the peat fields,
black as the faces of the local sheep that wander
like nomads on the high slopes forged half a billion
years ago and polished by patient glaciers.

Shifting shadows from scudding clouds race across
burnished bogs and on a faint blue horizon
Benbulben sits swathed in haze. I hear my grandfather's
tones, as rich as this fertile carpet, gentle and spiritual,

yet strong and earthy. I see anonymous ancestors
stretching silently into the ghostly mist that hangs
over the copper hedgerows and the yellow gorse
and the white hawthorn, like abandoned laundry.

It is a narrative of human survival. But more than all that,
it is where my roots were nourished and endured.
Among the buried bones and reposing memories
this is my home.

Ian Chambers

For My 90th Birthday[16]

For my 90th birthday I want
a pair of spiked running shoes,
green like the ones I had at school,
to remind the staff that I was once
a human being, alive and athletic,
not just something to keep them busy.

I'd also like copies of the autobiography
that I should have written, so that everyone
will know that I am not empty, that I have
done so much more than they could ever
imagine, learned so many of Life's lessons,
made and survived so many mistakes
that could have been, but thankfully
weren't avoided.

Lastly, I would like a large framed photograph
for the main entrance. Not some faded
sepia family wedding or anonymous office
image but a shot of me pole-vaulting or
graduating from Cambridge or escorting
the Queen or landscaping our Annapolis garden,
to remind visitors that this place should not
be seen as a repository of spent shells
but as a place of slower lives; that I was
once able to hunt and gather instead of
being sat in front of endless TV game shows
to keep me quiet until my next birthday.

Ian Chambers

The Dying of the Light[17]

The midnight phone call ended
and sleep was suspended.
I imagined you lying oblivious,
faltering, precarious
in that alien bed, your
penultimate resting place,
all but pain control rejected
through your own foresight.
Despite the intractable miles,
I felt close, connected.
Your unsettled breathing
became mine and I thought
of that distant beginning
when we last breathed as one,
when I lay, as now, wombed
in darkness, my heartbeat
driven by yours.

When the phone rang again
we were no longer
together.

Ian Chambers

Words[18]

They fall, float, catapult
through the air, from body
to body in light or dark,
love or anger, with awesome
nothingness; abstract beings
that can skulk behind concrete
glyphs distracting and shaping
our thoughts, not dead yet buried
in mankind's fabric, upon
the stone hardness of sun-starved
caverns, upon transient hosts
that decay beneath their content,
in the grandfathered tales
of the seanachaí, or now
disseminated through the
speed-of-light ether.
I have used them to document
a cluttered now dusty life,
to try to coalesce meaning
and objectivity, even salvation.
And I have used them to paint
your cheeks with the dampness
of a love left hanging, using
their uncompromising power
like a wildly wielded knife
to vent my red-rag rage—
as though *they* give a damn.

Ian Chambers

Under the Blue Tarps[19]

You could probably see them from space
The tarps that cover the broken rooftops
Some from bombs some from wind and fire
The patchworks of blue that pinpoint disaster

I've seen them filling in the blanks
Of the burnt orange tiles of Dubrovnik
Just after the siege when the mortars
Left craters on the shining marble streets

They were everywhere in New Orleans
Covering the holes where some escaped
From attics using axes and butcher knives
As the waters rose and it was life or death

In the town of Paradise they blanketed
The smoking ruins of dreams and lives
Lost or interrupted and what was left
Of the promise of always good weather

After fire, hurricane, tornado or flood
They arrive as shelter from the storm
Suggesting that camping isn't so bad and
That the sound of rain on plastic is pleasing

If not anchored the ends of the tarp flap madly
Like manta rays finding themselves on the beach
These inorganic unlovely stand-ins for real cover
Supposedly temporary but often there 'til they rot

I imagine that someday we will all know that fake blue
Above our heads that flaps and fades in the sun
As we lose the sense of safety we thought we held
As the waters keep rising and the winds keep blowing

Carol Flake Chapman

On One Out-Of-The-Way Thing[20]

If I were
To expect out-of-the-way things
To one day occur, I'd say I'd hear
Your gloomy soul charming in singing
Of rhymes dipped in soft honey drops,
And the wind chiming your murmur with ringing.

And if you were
To stride matter-of-factly but with grace
Finally to close up the miles apart
Between the dripping dew on a sunflower and the
nightingale's race,
Oh, how hushed would be the sound of fall
That awaits the thirst of one, long lost, many a day.

And if we were
To savour two-in-one bitterness and sweetness
To behold the wintry and the warm
Whilst I was your witness
And you were mine
In this vast phantom of fleetness ...

But, alas for me!
It will never be true
For your singing tongue shall never be heard;
A nightingale shall never dance in the midnight blue;
And your heart shall not be mine to own;
For out-of-the-way things exist only upon pillars of hue.

Fiona Chen

"Appearances" from *Criminal Cipher Code for Police Officers* [21]

Male Usual,   Will they work around us slowly?
        Make (one's) Bones   Did you tell them women will be there too?
                Man Nod,   Should they rise and squat to your pulse rate?
Mattress Worship,   What part of the couple's bodies exited the salt circle?
        Meat market,   How many people can fit in this hotel room bathroom?
                Message Anxiety,   Can the floor handle this?
Methamerican,   How can I fill the puncture hole?
        Mickey,   How much confidence do they have in their own race?
                Midnight Auto Parts,   Did you say "shhh" when they stepped on the line?
Milkman,   Do they think of us when there is a release of pressure?
        Mirror Meeting,   Will you maneuver your fingertips to keep them quiet?
                Model-Turned-Actress,   At what time did they throw back their heads?
Monkeyfishing,   Does he think my name is Lana?
        Monster,   What was his mindset when he inched towards the cone?
                Mother of Satan,   Is she dangerous when she gets bigger?
Munging,   Has this large plastic tube been used before?
        Murderabilia,   Did He get the bath he desired?
                My-Face-When,   How soon until this light of blessedness is enough?

Annie Christain

To carry on[22]

My feet carry
Me carrying
A backpack carrying
The many carry-ons
That allow me to carry on
One heavy solitary journey
As I carry on
To the end of the day
To the end of the journey
Carrying the hope that
Down the road somewhere
The journey carries at least one good story
One good show
To prove the travel's worth the trouble
And the load but a logo to laud in limbo
So I carry on
Praying that each day carries a guarantee
That there would be light at the end of each tunnel
And cheers through all the sadness and the sorrows
And so I carry on
My feet carrying
Me carrying
A backpack carrying
The many carry-ons
As life goes on
Carrying heavy memories of
All that I have carried
Courtesy of the One
Carrying the Cross through centuries
As Life carries on
With or without me

Teresa Ngan-fung Chu

Mermaid Tears[23]

From the beach house I watched
turbulent clouds rumbled out to sea
surf churned, nature's rock tumbler,
tossed then littered upon variegated sand
cowry shells, mussels, skate egg cases

Gulf Stream carried Lilliputian glass shards
buffed by years of tumbling in tidal waves
brilliant hues now frosted pastels
seafoam green bits of bottles
cobalt blue chips of jars

As high tide receded on Emerald Isle shores
I strolled the beach in search of treasures
glass story tellers harder to find
instead I collected plastic cups,
aluminum cans, and tangled fishing lines

Angered by trash that gagged Atlantic waters
my thoughts deepened like a sunken ship,
conscious excuses, debris, drifted on the surface
I struggled for solutions while undertows of
expense and practicality dragged me down

How long must my mind tread before
oceans are lost to irreparable deterioration?
I shed tears over damaged artifacts and polluted waters.

Suzanne Cottrell

A Memory[24]

I watch an impoverished woman on the screen
who watches
the sea for the first time without speaking
in the sound of waves
that mixes with her thoughts
beneath her sinuous veil of motifs surrounded
by grey water while thoughts are doubtless influenced
by the artist's device
and the instructions to follow
but some of those thoughts let themselves be defined
by new sensations
when a wave reaches the shore of awareness before
the woman turns around
and I leave the screen and museum
taking with me a faceless memory to work on
in the future forgetting of a one and only memory of the sea.

Stéphane D'Amour

The SOG[25]

The grey comes down, And takes you in,
You have a SOG. Sigh… there!
Everything descends into mud.
Get up! Do what? SOG chokes and traps
How to release? What can you do about this SOG thing?
Once you have it? Please?
Chase it out. Call up your force.
Go to the gym. Gain strength and size.
Feed it chocolate? Gain weight and caffeinate.
Have a G and T, do. Try a night in Soho for two?
Find a partner for your triple cheese pizza.
Run, run, run … A-do run, run.
Do what you will, You cannot banish the SOG.
The SOG is yours
Slink around it, Flow through it
Know it by its name. SOG!
It's through you and in your core You can forget about it
It will bite you on your Bum! Be warned!

As your companion SOG throws all in to relief,
For how to know your colours, If you don't have the grey.

You can have the lows, You can have the highs!
So keep it, don't ignore, Don't feed it too much
Know it doesn't like fresh air, Sunshine or changes of scene,
But it'll stay anyway.

It doesn't like good friends, companionship or casual
conversation
But it will stick around. Even as a dot on the horizon.

SOG!

Helen Davis

plasticine ιδέες[26]

wonder plants on the sidelines inhale the nervous air emitted
by neon. new is neon when all the way to the gutter time is
but a blur. and the blur, the slurring prediction of weather
vanes slithers through and across this and that 'thing' and
'non-thing' surface of disaster splitting in half the body.
rhizomatic moon-body. human or not, the body fragments,
fades in the grass until it becomes plastic. the beginning,
says the complacent poet-critic whose love for cats has been
admirable, like the body, the 'about us'-telex truth, is
impersonal. the moon is a room for. its bright treatment of
the rain wassails with. its people, all dressed in, singing to.
since rain seems plastic & ear-biting to the point of view of
dear trees, the moon predictably likens the body to the
natural habitat of signs, of neon drowning still the. *wonder
plants. perfumed by poetry or—philosophy.* the Ecosystem,
the still neon-twinkling thought of. the world: you & me &
this apparition of faces, Notre Dame burning out of time w/
Kreymborg flowers all phrasally rooted to the print
composition of 'vers libertines' in *Others*. where is the
Other in *The Waste Pound & Other Poems*? subjected to,
quarterly slicing open, the social subjectile: my dear abiotic
of the super blood wolf moon, Radiate ways of making
ideas colourfully new!

Lawdenmarc Decamora

Nan Lian Garden[27]

*"Where there are places for relaxation in the mundane
world, there is no need to live as a recluse in the
mountains"*
—Bai Juyi

This garden is managed by the Department of Leisure and
Cultural Services. Visitors are requested to abide by the
rules for their own enjoyment and the safety of others: no
bawling or brawling. No frolicking or running. No carving
of graffiti. No climbing on the rocks. No littering, hawking
or touting. No drinking except water and the breast feeding
of babies. No eating unless within designated areas. No egg.
No release of aquatic animals in the Lotus Pond. No bladed
instruments including scissors. No nail clippers. No
ceremonial swords or Swiss knives. No sighing, snorting,
spitting or loud chewing of gum. No shampoo or non-
prescription laxatives. No commercial or flash photography.
No tripods, video-shooting, self-shots or ring tones.

*The trees are Black Pine Buddhist Pine Cherry Orange
Jasmine
Silk Cotton Box Ash Fig Merrill Elm
And the Banyan grove is a cathedral in a concrete canyon
And the pagoda has no nails
But timber tongues and grooves
And the windows have no steel no glass
And the wood reeks of incense suffused by prayer
And the trees insulate the silence*

We aspire to the aesthetic of Truth in Beauty. Visitors are
requested not to wear clothes or any kind of costume that
would disturb the serene ambience.

Beneath vermillion bridges
The river flows East
And the gateway to heaven is carved with the Sun
The gateway is carved with the Moon
The lintel the clouds
The rocks are ancient memory
The skeleton for what breathes and grows
And curves and slopes and undulates

No feeding of fish or the snake. No playing with water or
the snake.
Do not pick the fruit.

The roof is the sky

Infinite

Blue

The toilets adjacent to the Pavilion of Absolute Perfection
are inspected every hour (30 minutes on Bank Holidays).

Please keep off the grass.

Neil Douglas

Odysseus' Farewell to Calypso

Won't you stay, just a little bit longer, she said,
her lips moist with nectar.
He gazed, outward,
to the green marbled sea.

It's been seven years, he said.
It's not you it's me, he said.
It's not you it's her, she said.
Her? he said.
Penelope, your wife, she said.
Oh, he said.

The salt air stung his eyes
giving the appearance of tears.

I offered you immortality she said.
Couldn't live with that he said,
and left.

Neil Douglas

Super blood wolf

I was told you would blush,
caught in the Earth's umbra
by the thick-cut love bite
of a marmalade sun.

The sky watchers said I would howl,
canines bared, as you swelled—
a fat plastic tomato ready to squeeze ketchup
on a tablecloth of stars.

But I was fast asleep, and you, obscured
by light pollution, a cloud.

Neil Douglas

**The Assassination of Comrade Trotsky, Mexico City,
August 1940**

Ramon Mercader, fox-sly Bolshevik,
laid his stone grey raincoat on the table
in such a way that he could take the ice pick
from the pocket where he had been able
to conceal it, gripped the steel, narrowed his eyes
to see his closed fist clenched white before the fall.
Trotsky thought: Life is beautiful. Blue skies
clear above the wall and below the wall
I can just see the bright green strip of grass
bathed in sunlight; all in sunlight, then
fingers the crack on his commissar's watch glass.
The sound of a skull split like a melon.
The red, the red pool spreading on the floor.
Natalia screaming, ashen, at the door.

Neil Douglas

The Courtship of the Mire Dromble

The Mire Dromble is a diffident bird—
quiet, secretive, he assumes nothing
as he stutters through the wetland,
a syncopation of pale plumage,
buff-brown streaks, scattered black bars,
keeping an almost rhythm with the sway of reeds
like a shy suitor fidgeting at the dance floor's edge.
But come the Spring he booms, bellows like an ox.
He is a bog-bull, a stake-driver, a full-throated thunder-
pumper.
And she, nonchalant, nested some distance across the marsh,
hears him, wonders if she is sufficiently impressed
to offer him her golden possibility
and skip the polite fandango.

Neil Douglas

Blue Mondays[28]

Can you remember walking around asleep?
Blue Mondays are naturally lazy,
Victims of their own inertia.
Grey skies make it possible to remove human responses.
Nature, using an algorithm, finds sleep conceivable.
Open the door into the link between human inadequacies.
Imagine—People winding their way with every passing day.
Squeezed, desperate sequencing.
It's easy to feel naturally lazy.

Jennifer Ann Eagleton

A Call from the Well[29]

The hound who killed me has a crown on his head.
Did you hear me? Is everyone also dead?
He sports a beard and a dashing desert smile,
You saw him in the middle of the picture,
A mixture of old tradition and new trend,
Posing like an innocent sinless woman,
Between the widening East and the shrinking West.

I know that my face must be expressionless;
My head was separated from my body,
But what went wrong with your petrified faces?
I know my body was cut into pieces,
But what has befallen your restrained bodies?
You seem to be whole, you're still in your places.
Perhaps what I said didn't make any sense?

Let me try this from collective memory:
The emperor has no clothes! How does this one sound?
Still no response? It doesn't ring any bells?
Well, if Hans Christian Andersen is now dead
In your head, if you have suppressed his free voice,
Then I can't expect mine to be heard, I guess
I'll say: Viva Trumpism! Viva the Prince!

Ahmed Elbeshlawy

The Message of the Music[30]

And so plays on the quartet.
Civilized and attentive,
The audience are transported
Through music to other worlds.

I'm fixated on the girl
With the bushy flaxen hair
In the fifth row. Music makes
People look more beautiful,
Like red wine, the problem is
I have to smile and be nice
Yet blithe, I must seduce her.

But that isn't the message
Of the music we're hearing.
The message is to go there,
Grab that bushy flaxen hair,
Pull her head up in the air,
Whisper, whisper in her ear
The vicious thoughts I'm having

And so plays on the quartet.
Civilized and attentive,
The audience are transported
Through music to other worlds.

Ahmed Elbeshlawy

21st Century Immigrant[31]

Our paper boat finally stabilised
After the storm
Only twelve of us drowned
This time.
The rest are determined to reach
A destination,
Any destination,
Except home.

Apiyo is smiling at me.

She is not dead,
I am not dead,
We might have a life ahead.
Her beauty overwhelms me.
Even after three days
Without food, her head
Is held high towards the sun
Like a golden black dome.

Apiyo is smiling at me.

The paper boat carrying
The black bodies sways
Chillingly.
My back touches the body
Of the deep blue creature
Sensually.
My eyes roam from my beloved
To the disappearing foam.

Apiyo is smiling at me.

She lets me see
The beauty of our bodies
And the body of the sea.
Home is within me,
Home is within me,
As long as her African hair
Glitters under the sky,
Filling my soul.

Apiyo is smiling at me.

At night, we sleep soundly
In spite of everything,
In close proximity
To fight the cold weather.
At night, I still have dreams.
At night, I still have erections
In spite of everything.
The world is still warm.

Apiyo is smiling at me.

This is our fifth day at sea.
I remember my English teacher
And that long poem;
"Water, water, everywhere,
And all the boards did shrink;
Water, water, everywhere,
Nor any drop to drink".

What was the name of the poet?
Salmon? Burger? Porridge?
Did he die in London or in Rome?
Ah, the European city,
The promised land.
The civilization haunting us
From our earliest days
Through images and words.

Apiyo is smiling at me.

"Eneo! Eneo!" shouts the man
At the bow.
Land finally appeared.
It looks mountainous,
It looks majestic,
It even looks sexy
Like a pair of proud breasts.
We found our new home.

Apiyo is smiling at me.

The mountains are getting nearer,
But there is a stench.
Is it us? Is it the sea?
Did the whale defecate?
It does not matter.
The mood on the boat is orgiastic;
We beat all the odds
And it was all quite fantastic.

Apiyo is smiling at me.

But the smile slowly slips into a sulk,
As we see the sickness of the sea.
The mountains are made of plastic.
Garbage, garbage, everywhere,
That made the wind skulk;
Garbage, garbage, everywhere,
Forming a huge filthy bulk
On the surface of the sea.

Apiyo stopped smiling.

Ahmed Elbeshlawy

American Seasons

Autumn, 1964,
western New York State:
walking the furrowed deer tracks
                out beyond the lip of the woods
on our way to play at Sonnenberg Park—

we believed those paths were Indian trails
            worn into the dirt, dividing the trees,
all the way out past a starry base of diamond
to the monkey bars, thick poles of iron
polished to a copper sheen
                    by legions of little hands.

We'd shimmy our willowed bodies
from side to side, then up and up,
            catch the swinging trapeze, or not,
landing hard in a cushion of dust
imprinted with elbow and knee.

One winter, the old Academy track
froze over so flawlessly, a seven-foot fence
was nothing between me and that perfect ice.
I skated 'til my ankles swelled against the leather boot—

the free glide and backward cross,
the same as Great-grandfather Jan
who stroked and flew his way
            over Amsterdam's canals,
            the city's frozen arteries—
one arm anchoring his aching back,
the other propelling him home,

just days before a late-spring thaw
                would bless his boat trip over—
before new lake-land revealed itself,
before the line was laced with Irish;
before Annie Laurie, his last surviving child,
would be conceived in the rancid hold
                of a transatlantic schooner.

                              *

I was ten *the Year of the Perfect Ice.*
By then, Annie Laurie was already old.
For forty-five years,
              she held the light dominion
over landscapes of brawlers, whispered liaisons,
the unborn, stillborn souls
disappeared from sound and sight.

Most nights, she pulled her husband Dickie
out from under barstools.
                              And every spring,
she scrubbed the winter sidewalks clean
the length of Telyea Street.

              Annie Laurie was tired.

A sullen March morning,
the day Annie Laurie didn't wake up,
              I turned twenty-one.
With no reason to stay,
I traded in those northern lights
              for sodden Novembers
and run-off straight to the Malibu pier,
for the Santa Anas' saw-edged blades,
              for nights full of rumble and crack.
                              *
A few miles north of the Hollywood sign,
the air thick with orange blossom,
streets well-lit, the traffic sparse,
                  I found a Spanish bungalow
with popcorn ceilings, paper-thin walls.

Today, the walls are tempered glass
to frame the hills surrounding,
their deepening shadows
              of loden green, indigo—

Nothing I have, nothing I own
can quell this craving for ochre,
            for orange,
            the leaves, the days—

my September song plays on and on
in deep, percussive tones that ring out
here in the west, my adopted home,

            and there, in the ever-rising east:

memories burnished by autumn's umber,
gilded with falling snow.

C.W. Emerson

All-Inclusive Guilt-Trip Getaway[32]

we want to swim in
the cerulean sea
bathe with our feet in
a pool of luxury
but the price of the boat
is its black plumes of smoke
and we aren't the ones
paying for it
at least not yet

it's the ocean picking up the tab
hourly for our habits
destructive to ourselves
and our habitat
the worst kind of addicts
we demanded
the world all-inclusive
one-time-use shampoos
and disposable toothbrushes

the floss we use
turns to turtle nooses
fishing line biting the fish who won't bite
dinner or
death with no
sustenance-excuses
killed by and for
our one-time-uses

and we don't call
our mothers anymore
we are at war
with who we used to be
using up the past 'til we don't know
where our food comes from or
who died so we could eat it

we've built a world of plastic
and remade ourselves to match it

and the sea
she
is running out
of money

Rayn Epremian

Choking Back Thirty Tears!

This papa did accurately
surmise undeclared war
strong armed lance pierced my armour,
ah...how fondly he recalls
early fatherhood days of yore,
when daddy's first born girl
did effusively adore
yours truly, he likened self as topnotch
trooper, who mustered vigour
exhibiting untrammeled unconditional
tender loving behaviour
before conflict erupted as between
mainland China and Uighur
back in the day din and clangour
honed, perfected, battle
tested... mine steely danse zing mettle
admirable trait evinced by this troubadour,
when understandable mutiny arose 'tween
me and "Munchkin" do not ask anymore,
why spouse described eldest
with pet name eldest she smoothly bore
intermittent flashpoints smoothed, sans
24/7 at beck and call, I availed to assuage
with papa's magical succor
distressed damsel (daughter number one),
she established an endearing rapport
with me telepathic sixth sense touchstone
oft times found even how sailors swore
dem crude words
extraneous, ridiculous, superfluous...

Matthew Harris

Takeaway Eaters[33]

Takeaway eaters
Are polluting our beaches
With plastic pieces.

Kate Hawkins

Advanced Plastic

In life, everyone gathers plastic:
plastic politics, plastic religions,
plastic media, plastic philosophies,
plastic socializing, plastic sex toys,
with all of it tarnishing our spirits.

Everything is plastic, which can be
bright or dark. You can sit on it,
stand on it, or eat it, nonetheless,
it's still plastic.

We are becoming hard plastic
like the Invisible Man or Woman
and when we fuck we'll produce
Invisible Babies with plastic hunger

and the Invisible Babies will give
plastic advice on how to wrap
the world in a more durable plastic
and how to build a state-of-the-art
heaven with a new plastic god

Dah Helmer

A Stranger On The Street[34]

He has been there since
the time
the city started to gentrify itself, bidding
a hasty goodbye
to its dubious past, when
people still believed
    the idea of a home.
Ten years maybe?
    or even longer—man
has to marvel at the amnesia,
   the new norm in this country, though mendacious
like propaganda.
    we tend to forget,
about people under the wheels
of a creakily-moving-forward
history.

    I know him
as the under-bridge man who builds his home
under an overpass that hangs
silently
like a broken flute
    above the city's monotonous din;
Maybe he could find peace there,
a scroll of dirty sheets;
  a bag with a few winter coats
(How he suffers the scorching summer!)
    and a bowl to collect money with.
    He lives
like a monk on offerings but WE,
who are notoriously less-trusting of the poor,
do not really see him as he falls deeper
and deeper into the shadow
of the wall.

We don't see many like him,
especially inside the inner-highway that surrounds
the downtown like a polluted moat,
staving off the "unworthy", who migrate everyday
like birds
    for the wheat field.
What crumbs do they gather?
What innocent money falls
from the gracious hands of the rich?
I can't tell—
there must be another way of living,
        a harsher way
that will bend most of us like a twig in winter,
then snap us away to make room
for the next generation
        of more practical men.

He is there,
    under the overpass,
hands stretching out like one thin bodhisattva
    man is afraid to look at;
Sometimes 5 RMB,
Sometimes half a pack of cigarettes,
Sometimes children spit in his palms;
—I
sit comfortably in the café; stories
of a thousand different lives might spill
from my pen,
    but none about him—
For literature pales at the thought
of human sufferings,
No words
can sufficiently describe the force
that twists our fate—I might be him one day,
and he'd sit inside this café,
contemplating, affectedly,
life's silent mockery

I have to give a proper ending
to my writing
and to his reality as well—one
that suits the current social climate.
(the weaponized teachings of the Analects, how
many times this happens!!)
I see the day when
the guard comes and whips him away
like a rodent,
his heart-rending cry, short
of a flawless argument that saves
—I,
like most of my fellow brothers,

only stand and watch.

Aiden Heung

At Dragon's Back, Hong Kong[35]

We feel beneath our feet
the force that antagonizes gravity, as
we haul ourselves
like two dirty cases and ascend
onto the steps of Dragon's Back;
our shadows follow like a vibration
from a long time ago, still
pulling, maybe a gentle reminder
of our untimely
presence here and now, when
the silence of the passing gulls is

incriminating
and our breath intertwines, hurried like pleas—
The rocks rise before us; an integrity
of the timeless grey
rolls out righteously

and suddenly the path turns
        to the sea,
            the blue sea,
drowned in its own blueness, quietly spreads

out from the mountain mouth where
the wind slumbers; I halt
and watch these houses that scatter
down there like mural pieces, patiently
inviting a new ode from a young poet,
a mark on the map suggesting a triumphant
discovery—but I forget

that we are far from home, both you and I,
we have no right
to claim this shore, to call it our own. we
are footnotes to a different story;
but I call out anyway like a spoiled child,
throwing echoes
among the cliffs that run alongside us,
"heyyyyyyyyyy-hoooooo",
there comes back to me, another kind

of greetings, an explosive unity, an appeal
to my seething blood almost bleached
by a totalitarian sun; all my ideals
become dynamic; I

am free
like the space that suddenly opens up
on the mountain ridge and I

am no less certain of where my steps might take me.

Aiden Heung

Salvation[36]

The incense burns late in this grand temple
by the sea where the sea is muzzled, tamed,
as if the godly force became timely
diplomatic, now a peaceful face, gilded and veiled,
barely blushing at the fawning smoke that rises
with a metallic odour.

I stand at the gold-studded gate,
knowing not if I should go in,
hesitant like a schoolboy.
Busy tourists swarm behind me
and wave entrance tickets like praying flags;
while the guard,
like a deity at the heavenly gate,
petulantly gathers the offering—

30 RMB, that's the price of salvation.

Aiden Heung

How to Build a Living Skyscraper[37]

Lay the foundation of faith.
Construct walls made of dream bricks,
Glued together with your determination
To live life to the fullest.

Build opportunity elevators,
That lead to floors of new experiences.
Add chimneys
That emit optimism.

May your living skyscraper
Inspire others
To rise above hopelessness,
And capture every joy star,
That life has to offer.

Elmira Hooper

Peace Offering

Hear God's peace
Singing around you.
Let it enfold you
In its warm blanket.

Let your soul
Breathe the oxygen of peace,
And release the carbon dioxide
Of stress and tension.

In the crazy cacophony
Of fast paced existence,
Rest in prayerful tranquility.
Then peace will rest in you.

Elmira Hooper

The Whispering Wind's Serenade

The wind whispers
A spring serenade
To awaken the hibernating earth.

Soon that gentle whisper
Will become a joyful chorus
As the air resonates
With returning robins,
And forests, fields, and trees
Lift their aromatic voices
To welcome the spring.

Elmira Hooper

Invasive Species[38]

i.
My last, best, unstraight-laced ditchdigger
carried consternation over Jesus, LSD, and
Robert Lowell off to Nepal; there, she
painted Gods all in human skins, advised
dialogue over plot, and got shaped by tragedy.
She painted mornings' mountains out so far,

ii.
her dreams no longer felt their legerdemain.
A thousand winds blew through her each night.
She elbowed out a tiny niche, dug deep latrines,
dug deeper wells, their bottoms nearly mica mines.
At twenty-three, pearl tampons ferried by monthly air.
No lovers; village elders nixed comingled strains.

iii.
She strides within her iridescent bubble, gazing over
sloping tides of scree—slick, glossy, treacherous, and
fetishized. Scarves, scarves twirl about her hot neck,
scattering tiny, alien passengers across the discotheque.
Barring grace, her *Be equals?* curtsy might be querulous;
her *I want to dance to your rock-'n'-roll* clashes with
    Sarowar.

iv.
Early on, she'd anticipated some spring—sure, or bounce—
but not this quixotic, subtle or not, tug-of-war
as in-country rectors civilly unsoftened their edges.
Wasn't it the *Age of Exploration*, she'd alleged?
Wasn't there some jointly happy shore? She thought
she'd ordered Vichyssoise—instead got Borscht.

R.J. Keeler

A Monolith to Demeter[39]

an apology slipped from my lips
crooked are my teeth, you can't believe me
I raked the sands of Omaha beach
to find peace

how could I not remember?
my darling, Demeter
with so many phantom memories knocking at
my temple doors

I didn't mean to mistreat her
I never could have known she gives
as well as she takes

I polluted her rivers
trashed her seas
murdered her trees
stripped her bare for all to see
robbing her of precious metals
and gems for money

I pushed her too far
brought her to her knees
to beg for mercy
all in the name of progress
all for the sake of industry
all to make someone else money

I am starting to think it was all a mistake
she quakes with fury, storms lash out from the sky
she's turned up the heat, she's left us to fate

she won't talk to me anymore
no matter how many calls or pleas I make
even in the old days her proud, smug vanity
emitted beauty and my arrogance only breeds
ugly wasteland, houses that resemble tin cans

where am I to go now that no one wants me around?

I'll go back to the place where thought springs
cleanse me of these sins not to forget but to do better
I'll meet my maker
I'm afraid, I don't want to leave anything behind
come abyss.
I'll greet you with a kiss
we'll laugh again like reuniting with an old friend

I'll leave a gift as I go from Demeter
a monolith to mark the love she and I once made
and engraved upon it
"I was too weak to fall into your arms
You were too strong to remind me"
I am sorry, I will say as I take my leave
please forgive me but don't forget

Zachary Knox

cut over the eye

I got scratches down the length of my spine
a landmine somewhere deep in the recesses
there is some attachment I can't find
if I crack the code
I know the golden yolk inside will break
it's in there waiting, longing to breed
with the orgy air
who loses when no one does?
all the failures needed was a hug
I'm told someone, somewhere gives a fuck
frankly, to be perfectly honest, I don't want to
push my luck
fortune favours the failure
only the brave eventually succeed
if you want to know learn to read
if you want to understand learn to bleed.

Zachary Knox

electric light

there's a ghost in the lights
it talks in a flickered code
the city I live in chokes on the smell of death
breathe in deep the second hand air
with enough time the stench will disappear
you will no longer be aware
the evidence will remain near

strange storms flood the sky
ashen snow will fall overnight
it's in the cold one understands life
winter is a heartbeat, summer the pulse
spring is where things come to die
flies swarm around the pupil
of the third eye

under the porch plead reality
for a divorce
the smokestack on the edge of town
is hungry
another life will soon burn down in the furnace tonight
feeding the land of strife with light
the charge is in the air it almost appears like life
it slithers through the wire
sleeps on a mattress made of hair

a man's home is his palace
his kingdom a cage
the knight of shades is coming
better keep the meter running
and escape before you become brave
make the ghost pay the electric bill if it wants to stay

Zachary Knox

sober moments

I stare down the neck of a beer bottle
it's a spyglass to see into the shattered
fragments of me
I wander here and there
demons wear human skin
scalped women and men
line the backdrop of my dreams
nightmares are bred from plight

I eat bread to put me to sleep
the body under the floor snores loudly
I dismember each moment
between nights
can't find it
commercials on tv try to sell me a lifestyle
someone I could be
I don't mind it
because I don't think there even is a
me although I talk about him recreationally

Zachary Knox

The Great Divide

there's division in the streets
show pride and pick a side
dredge the river
the dead will decide
although who knows
what they mean
they speak in parables
and a language from
the land of dream

I used madness to escape it all
answers here are currency
there was none to be found
some body hacked into
my bank account
and emptied it out
it's easy to be mad without money
people judge and say I'm lazy and want a hand-out
I say,
the banker can lend me the cash to pay
the lease
they will give me the aids with an attached interest fee
owed is owned until what is loaned is paid back

Zachary Knox

Anticipated arrival of a Predicted blizzard[40]
With appreciation to Dr Ann Paton for an E-mail
conversation which inspired this poem.

Sitting in my office
taking care of business
in Wurtemburg, Pennsylvania

Two gray cats watch birds from open window.
My dogs and I are out the door before dawn. They sniff
trails on woodland paths, track deer.

I search for fragile lavender phlox
swaying in morning breeze.

My husband cooks hot oatmeal in the kitchen.
He stops to comment on country
Songs on radio.

"I can't understand the words," he says.
But, I know he's hard of hearing.

My friend, Ann,
sent me a copy of her Easter sermon
about Moses and his encounter
with a burning bush.

Since then, I keep wondering
what sort of bush is it?
Perhaps it is a Privet bush
like the ones here in my woods.
Maybe a Red Barberry Bush
with drooping red berries
still hanging on it after a long winter.

I wonder, "what makes a bush worthy
of Divine inhabitation."

Why did she tell me
she thinks I am a burning bush?

Now, I worry that God might jump
inside of me some day when I am walking my dogs
or when
I stop to touch the delicate phlox?
Or, is God already inside of my body?
If that is the case.
can anyone see me glowing?

Looking back to Moses.
We enter the story with its only human character, Moses.

Think where he is.
Geographically
out beyond the wilderness.
That's far out!
And that's where he is personally.

After lunch,
I'm going to take off my sandals.
Just like Moses,
I'm looking for a burning bush.

Sitting in my office
taking care of business
in Wurtemburg, Pennsylvania

Lynda Lambert

Hades' Song[41]

Fate happens quickly.

I snatched love
(My big surprise!)
she
plucked a flower
from my hot hand

we struggled

Filched destiny
Is a fragile obsession

I want to protect you.
Reach for my hand!

Feel my hot-blooded passion
warm your body through
endless night—
comfort you
surround you with ardour.

We traveled swiftly
through daydreams,
seasons,
nocturnal sunsets.

Let me wipe away your fears.

It's impossible to answer
questions
about a life
we never knew.

Is a question of love

Interminable?

Lynda Lambert

Persephone's Song

A solitary flower
pale, golden lavender
like Byzantine silk
paper-thin, a fine blossom—
I float in a whisper of chiffon
turn slightly
in pale heliotrope light.

My eyes scan the field
as we sing
pluck tender spring flowers
from willow-green stems

Strange. This changing.
The descent—unexpected.

In his scarlet chamber
I search the ashes
for my bridal dress.

Unfathomable.

Lynda Lambert

Spill those Beans![42]

All my loves have been unrequited:
Country, family and bitterly yes, the stage,
But there remains one friend by whom I'm always invited,
Who can pull me out of my cage,
Who's always there for me, whenever I feel blighted
(That's all the time), helping me turn even life's most
difficult
page.

You get me out of bed in the morning,
And putting depression aside, my fears you assuage,
You revive me when over work I'm yawning—
Just by pouring….

How can Switzerland say you're not essential to life?
Don't give me that strife!
You make me face the day.
What more can I say?

Though you're just addiction and can't replace treading the
boards
Nor fill that hole in my heart, made by unrequited love's
swords,
Cappuccino, espresso, macchiato, corretto—
Coffee! At least *you* are always *perfetto!*

Susan Lavender

Plastika[43]

My seatmate looked at my little language book
so I told her that I always learn the language
on the plane heading for the country
in which that language is spoken.
She said, That is the most preposterous statement
I have ever heard. I said
But it's true. Oh, I don't learn to
really speak the language, just to say
stuff like Do you have a room? How much?
Where's the bathroom? Please. Thanks.
But that's a lot of language. So
I got off the plane in Athens, hailed a cab
and said Constitution Square. Blank.
So I said Syntagma, and away we went.
Study paid off. I'd learned the Cyrillic alphabet, too.
Ahead of us, a truck. A word painted on the back,
so throughout the ride, I laboriously translated pi,
lambda, alpha… into our ABC's. And,
and of the ancients, glory that was Greece, it said:
PLASTIKA. Plastics.
Like Greece itself, another glorious contribution
that has changed the world.

Iris Litt

Vent Love

Before me, I see rubberized plastic
limbs pumped up like pink sausages
bearing children's mitted hands,
and a rouge knock-off Faberge purse
humming between her legs.
A chucking in my throat recalls windows
blown into shape, a kind regurgitation
of peeping tommery I pursued
at ten years old, a taste for which
I've since dummied up.
Inhaling deep, my lungs fill with the giddiness
of model glue, an odour overwhelming
as I descend into this plasticized love
doll, her O-mouth shaking above me,
blue eyes frozen in open fury
like a carousel animal
while our skins kiss and squeal.
I don't yet know her name. (But she's made in America.)
Welcome to my world, I whisper,
in her voice, born again.

Wayne Mattingly

And Then Eve[44]

And so God formed the first woman
out of old carpet and recycled plastic,
took a thousand bottles out of the ocean,
gathered colourful particulates, melted them down,
injection molded her ten fingers and ten toes.
He bouqueted the carpet fiber to make her hair,
carved away her sharp seams, smoothed her curves,
and 3D printed her heart out of hard, breakable plastic.

And so He tilted her upwards, straight and rigid.
Her eyelids lifted; she explored in her body
and found her fingertips held moon shapes,
her ears could echo ocean sounds,
and her nose could smell snow coming,
even her tongue could taste the flesh of an apple.
Thoughts flooded through her in a painful awakening.

She realized that she existed only by force;
she could bend if he bent her.
She could speak if he spoke for her.
She could pray when he prayed for her.
She could chew and swallow if he fed her;
she could bite back if he bit her,
but she learned to smell fear all on her own.

Brittany Mishra

Dothead Missions

a single dothead left on the bed,
measuring time giving head.
loves strange labors, pulling free,
beacons of hope. Gravity.

cavities open under shared teeth
sucking under kisses,
flailing speech.
'dropping phones now and fuck off' are modern war cries
criminally conjoined, distant dreams.

fusillades of petrol spark plugs
fart and die
surrendering to your whims
far away, replicating
an overflowing gutter.
your Freson of laughter,
berets worn as plastic. Garter.

Variegations, variations, tampons at the beach
motorbikes with sweepers consciences of spleen.

Cavorting couples hide under bushes of half fumigated
release
you and me. we cry, and we search. we lie, and we perch.

One needs sang-froid to sing in the rain
One needs an umbilical cord, to toe the grain

you throw in your towel
your garbled release!
you throw in your towel
our story never ceased.

Rony Nair

Plastic Floats

your voice is hidden, far away in myth
shrouds, of overarching freeway, guilt ridden pith,
we elope into playpens to dream
of secure beats. newer rummages, newer dreams.

your treadways stay perched minus triptychs,
where once you cavorted, ledges now hide,
We walked over walls amnesiac, nightdresses slide,
glossing over elliptical cajoles,
fuming over voices spent.

you were always one to take it dumb slow
veritas, singled out. whisky trails in solitary pens,
screaming thoughts on Garnett bends.
carotid strands of light streak past circular oblongs,
festooned bus stops.

You once used to sit on those footstools.
alone.

Rony Nair

Indian summer

Chennai sauna
Kitchen
Air dense as dahl
Diced mango light
Dappled
Window shutters
Fans
Languid pulpy beat
Sullen
Ceiling shadows

Henna hands
Holding
Sanskrit page
The Gita
Absorbed
Through open pores

Keith Nunes

Nuclear ponderings—forgotten victims[45]

Pasifika peoples across the glistening span
Marshall Islands, Bikini Atoll, Rongelap, Mururoa…
the names still resonate in my brain
far-flung islands studded across the great Pacific
(ah, the irony of *that* name
witness rather to such duplicity, trauma
destruction of homes and lives
land cracked, air and sea poisoned
jellyfish babies just one of the legacies)
…islanders linked not only by Pacific surge and swell
but by shared subjection
to legally-sanctioned crimes
Bikinians, forcibly removed, five times relocated
a lifetime of tinned fish, nomads on alien shores
ever longing to return home—
"indefinite displacement" the official term…
voices too small and inconsequential
to ever garner the world's outrage
governments too powerful to be forced
to acknowledge guilt and shame …
who will heed such a small cry for justice
lost among the rising pleas from Manus, Christmas Island,
Nauru…
lost in the morass of troubled waters
that we navigate today

Helen Oliver

Many Horizons

The alley near my house, strewn with sodden wrappers,
the shimmering mirage of an oasis in the desert, shadowy
     Bedouin amongst palm trees.
My future self.
That moment of recognition when we first looked at each
other.
Villa Rufolo, standing in its Garden of the Soul, gazing
     entranced by the Bay of Naples, merging
into the endless topaz enormity of it.

Limitless ocean
Far as the eye can see, I
Glimpse the I within

Patience O'Neill

Seashore[46]

I splash through the seashore's edge, lick drops of seawater
from my face,
feet making soft sand-prints. Feel the surf as it curls around
my ankles.
See sleek sticks of driftwood, fishnets, buttons, toy spades,
razor shells, marbled stones polished by tides,
breathe in the reeky seaweed smells.
I stride into the wind, cheeks ablaze.
The joy of beachcombing.

Patience O'Neill

Sicily: A Haiban

We see the broken stones of the past
remnants of power, now strewn on arid soil, faiths of
centuries pass.
We stop to wonder at these fragments. Are we like them?
Invisible roots reach deep into the red earth of our shared
origins
our foundations.
Conquerors came—Phoenicians, Greeks, Goths, Arabs,
Byzantines, Normans—
such flowering of artistry and power. Square tombs, huge
temples, sacrificial altars,
mosaic story-boards alive with movement.
See how the conquerors became the conquered.

We yearn to belong
Boasting our supremacy
Then return to dust.

Patience O'Neill

Gentleness[47]

I look whole.
My smile wide.
But speak soft words.
One heated breath
And like a flake of snow,
I melt and become no more….

Rena Ong

Lullaby for a man[48]

My love wraps round your heart
My son, my little one, my man
It wraps around as gentle as
The sunlight moves across the hills
Removing winter and its chills.

My love enfolds the hurts
My son, my little one, my man
It envelops round, as hard as steel as
The armour of a gentle knight
Deflecting arrows and swords of might.

So, take heart
My son, my grown-up man.
No lie can penetrate the truth of love
No force can remove this from your heart
Nothing else matters as much
Than you are loved…always

Rena Ong

Silence[49]

The Sound of Silence
When no-one listens.

Words fill the air like the unobserved
Murmuration of birds.
Wildly flying, circling and turning as one.
Nature longing to show its glory.
Yet, fleeting, dissolving, dispersed…ignored.

Rena Ong

We Are Plastic
Twelfth Night

Blue curtains, white sheets, smell of antiseptic,
this is a transfer station
to my abyss of uncertainty.

A nurse came,
putting a black plastic film
onto my jade bracelet.
I started to feel anxious.

A chaplain came,
praying for strength and support for me.
Her voice is the warmest and gentlest
you could imagine,
reminding me of the music played by
an angel.

Nothing moves in the room,
except for the clock.
Time is never so slow,
and close
to me.

Finally, the operating room
I am in.
A dose of anesthetic,
I fall in my abyss, immediately.

Waking up,
I am back to the transfer station.
Nurses pass by,
saying words floating high.

The plastic film,
you can tear it off now.
Looking down to my abdomen,
I see it—the s-c-a-r,
glued by p-l-a-s-t-i-c.

Under the scar,
where the lump abode,
there is another mass,
made of ultreprec…protere…
which sounds like,
plastic to me.

Touching my skin,
I feel
I am plastic, and
we are plastic.

Jun Pan

We are Plastic
Macbeth

In the sky,
where birds fly high,
airplanes now drop by.
Products of artificial substance
attract seabirds, pigeons, and even sparrows
as food, and
strangle them
to death.

In the sea,
where fish swim free,
ships now drive in, with
grotesque human glee, and
bags, bottles, and even bait
that are made of organic polymers.
Fish, crabs, shells, shrimps …
They don't know.
They eat them all.

On the land,
where animals shake a human hand,
garbage trucks put together a weird band;
among their deliverables,
the marvelous inventions of humankind
are made of those synthetic compounds we everywhere find.
Cattle, sheep, goats, pigs …
They can't tell.
They become consumers of all.

When devouring birds, fish and animals
on our dining table,
are we, the greatest predators of the planet,
feasting on food
or our admirable innovations of
p-l-a-s-t-i-c?

Jun Pan

We Are Plastic
The Tempest

Human brains are plastic.
Human activities shape the development of human brains.
—Cheng Kai-Ming

With shining dresses, name, and
fame, you landed
to this soil
that you have so many questions about.
—curious Meorge.

We thought you were just curious.

Till one day,
you started to yell, shout and
lose control,
spreading your fury,
to every corner of the room.
—jealous Meorge.

I thought you were just jealous.

It was only a prelude.

We were born to this world,
with our brain
shaped by our experience, people
we think important to us, and even
the temperature.

We love, hate, and
envy others,
who moulded our
temper, character and
identity.

Harmony, happiness, and
humanity, last for
a glimpse of time.
There is no chance for you
to mourn the loss of
a normal human relationship.

We are
plastic. Human relationship is
plastic.

In the hustle and bustle of
this vulgarity, we sculptures—
chiseled by nature and culture—
follow the rules to
survive, and gradually,
lose our
self.

Under the glories of tuxedos and
evening gowns,
craziness and madness blow up
a game of
golf.

After the gale of chaos, it becomes
clear to me, that
goodness is not
yesterday's grief,
but a religion
that we hold onto as
belief.

Jun Pan

The Call

Silence, words, the message
Train, car, motorbike
Drawing towards
The Call

Last time we met
You cranked in the sofa
I held your hand
Neither knows what to speak

Three years of company
A lifelong concern

I sat there
Looking at you
Thinking of the days
You sat there
Watching us
Like a drama

Now
You have moved away
To answer your Call
Leaving us
To ours
Yet to fall

Jun Pan

Beach

Something that no one needs anymore, an empty vessel,
lying   on the shore.
No one's property, though someone paid for it.
In another time, place, the average package accrues fantastic
      value (water can be carried
over great distances) but now it belongs to everyone and no
      one. No one wants it.

When you have that unnerving sensation floating on the
surface   of the awesome waters
rubbing against an unidentifiable, slimy thing, provoking an
      instinct to flee,
that ruined bag or tarp has, in fact, returned to haunt you.
You might as well bathe in what you have accumulated, are
      accumulating.

This will be your unpaid job, since cash is already
calculating   the mess.
The economy forgot to compensate for an attractive
package, an empty vessel.
You sweep along the beach, collecting the biggest pieces,
those   glaring objects
opposite to rot, synthetics that are indeed dead, but refusing
to   relinquish their skull.

Bag the plastic, glass, styrofoam, the brightly coloured bits
and pieces that betray
a manufactured origin. The elements (salt water, sun) work
on   shoelaces, wires just as avidly
as if they were wearing down boulders. But plastic, as we all
      know, is unrelenting, breaks
but doesn't dissolve, challenging the thoroughness of
      volunteered labour.

This unskilled job, a job that anyone can do, won't be paid
for, but the actual value
(collecting the trash, sweeping the floor, swabbing the bowl)
is   priceless.
That is why you do it for free. It is an aimless creative task
akin   to reading a book
while basking in the sun before you jump in the water: Why
        would you do that?

In terms of payment, note the outcome. You have made
some   space for all those things
that have little need for a plastic bottle. It is now up to you
to   track the debris, displaced from
the beach. Toss something from the open window of a
moving   car, throw some
fragments into your garden. At least, then, the pile will be
more evenly
        distributed.

Andy Peyrie

Merri Creek—Brunswick East, Melbourne[50]

atmosphere weeps
giant powerlines
zap zap zap
although the birds
have already assimilated

rubbish tinsel
coils around branches
and supermarket ghost bags
lurk
as though the air is all plastic
sticking to lungs

when there's no rain
there's no flushing
away
and creek turns into moat beneath
Brunswick Terminal Station—
a high voltage fortress
emitting electromagnetic
radiation

it won't be long
before we hold a Doppler
over her swollen belly
and its heartbeat
will be gone

Martin Jon Porter

Marina

For Marina Cvetajeva, an exiled Russian poet

1.

When I write poems at night, you wake up,
because I am not here. But I want you
to wake up because actually, I am here
like back then, before we had our son.
Through that ceiling, we'll be able to see the stars soon,
you laughed when you looked up then,
we felt warmer for a while. After all, I can see
them, I can see them already. Cassiopeia,
signs. My restlessness, my passion,
how much have we got lost?
When you leave, I break through the yard,
and let the stars and the beasts in.

2.

How can you claim this is our
house? The beasts lurk in silence,
in their make-belief tameness, and when
you leave for the train in the morning,
I desire salt, that's how much I wish to quench
my thirst. I see my lover to
the platform, the coat whiffs,
but it's me leaving the compartment, all
illuminated. Free, free, free.

3.

Seriously, how can you claim this
is our house? The eternity of temporary solutions.
Isn't this also comforting?
When I'm feeling my worst, I keep reminding myself:
I am only visiting here and can leave whenever
I like. Fine, I'll say nothing.
I don't want to do any more translations. I don't want to
move again, almost certainly for worse.

At night I went out, the icy glaze
hardened like an omen. Cracks, crevices.
What for, who for am I waiting here,
right now, barefoot, chilly, in the concrete yard?

Simona Rackova
Translated by Natalie Nera

Remembering Snow[51]

its dendritic flakes
each a six-part forest
in miniature

its crackle on my tongue
a *menuet* of disappearance
without a coda

its bluish whiteness
laced with soft gold
in the evening sun

24th January, 2019

Joanna Radwańska-Williams

The Life Cycle of a Beach Ball[52]

Oh! I am lost at sea.
How did I get here? Bright orange
streaks fast as meteors, my stripes
blend into flame, hot hands touch me,
bounce, bam, buoyant, blown
away by a breeze, here I am! where?
The waves have lulled me.

How long has it been? I can't know.
Why is my orange fading? Will I turn green?
My shape, sagging, something has gone wrong.
The air is flowing out of me. Bubbling then
sinking, oh, no, where is the sun?
I have no movement left
of my own, only the water's tongues.

Can hardly speak now, fragmentary
stripes and shards of me
coming apart
such a shape-shifter, dis-
integrate, how can we re-
assemble, not now
it is too late.

Like Morse code, small dots, dashes
an SOS at sea.
Some dots are orange specks
some almost formless. No identity.
We're being swallowed, buried, minced.
Fish ingest us but we are not freed.
Amalgamation. End. Does this end?

May 15th, 2019

Joanna Radwańska-Williams

The Pendant[53]

The exoskeleton
        of a sea creature
        calcified red and pink
        coral
        the allure
            of Nature's bounty
            smooth and lucent

            handled with love
By an artisan
        who bought it from a fisherman
        who may have bought it from a diver
        who may have cut the creature open
        not for its flesh
            for its bone

            so unlike our own bone
            so perfect
            a created gem
             needing no alteration

            and yet transformed
      by expert hands
      carved oval
      set with diamonds
hung on a gold
        chain

How I admire it
        in its display case! enhanced
        vibrant
        ready to be worn

A tear of blood.

May 9ᵗʰ, 2012

Joanna Radwańska-Williams

Fresh Start[54]

Seasons change, times change
Bidding adieu, welcoming the new,
Looking for pristine possibilities,
Wheeling it over.

The gentle breezes
Ease out a very soothing farewell
As the leaves gently glide down
From thick treetops.

Bright-coloured seeds and leaves
Warm up dormant dreams
And deck up the dawning hopes
Deep deep within.

Revisiting the dream lanes
Colouring the long lost thoughts
Wishing for a time freeze
Of everloved moments,

Life is all about walking past
With good old times,
Racing forward with aspirations,
Hoping for prayers to be answered!

C.N. Rajalakshmi

Vishnu, The Preserver and Protector[55]

Bright and fresh
Another day unwinds
The slumbering world awakes
Serene and calm
Lord Vishnu on Aadi Sesha,
Quietly witnessing the lives lived...
The lighted lamp
Reflecting and radiating peace
The aroma of incense and flowers
Powerful vibrations of chanting
Whirling smoke from the incense
Rise and traverse up
Up where the Lord is
The preserver and protector
Resonating with spiritual rejuvenation
The atman or the being in us is energised

Lord Vishnu on Aadi Sesha
Easing it out for all souls
Like the snake moving out of its
Dead skin

Discarding troubles and worries
With the hood spread out
Encompassing the whole universe.
Lord Vishnu on Aadi Sesha
Fulfilling dreams
Anchoring faith and belief
Shouldering universal burdens
The vibration
Still echoes...
I am the preserver and protector.

C.N. Rajalakshmi

From the rooftop[56]

The damp wind knocks
at the city walls
asking to be let in
to peel away its colours

A careful rumble crawls
through the streets
looking for places to hide
in every gap it finds

Caged lights leap from
stacked windows of homes
to light up the night
and form shadows below

Despite the distant drilling
and the blinding lights
we remain at peace
as we sip at fresh tobacco
watching the heavy air
hold up the sulphur sky

Harsh Ramchandani

Myrrh[57]

The three kings sauntered in
with gold, frankincense and myrrh
like big shots, but what was a
rough-hands carpenter to do?
It was like giving a $100 bill
to a Lithuanian immigrant Stock
Yards laborer. It was stolen from
him by a bar owner who was in
cahoots with the pols.

        "Here's your change for a one."
        "I gave you a $100 bill."
        "Where would you get a $100 bill?"

Everything that was unfair
happened to Jurgis. Jesus
was just killed. It was a kind
of suicide since he became
flesh to die. So do we all.

We enter the jungle
and make our way
as far as we get, and,
then, it's over. Or is
it? Do we eat ice cream
in a vanilla heaven? Or
have dancing girls? What
do dancing girls get in
heaven? Ice cream?

The seed dies and finds
its heaven as a flower.
It has its own sweet
aroma and beauty.

Patrick T. Reardon

Sighting Polaris

*Wholesale displacement may be inevitable; but we should
not suppose that it occurs without disastrous consequences
for the earth and for ourselves.*
    —Scott Russell Sanders,
    Staying Put, Making a Home in a Restless World

My father, when lost, sought Polaris—star-shine surpassing
luminous sun—his symbol of love and home. Polaris,
sighting my father, set him to "making a home in a restless
world"—what would be his life-long labour of love. An
architect under St Patrick's wings, he transformed with
Mayo the hospitals into homes, redolent-Rumi gardens and
hospitality's arts.

Imagine being a young teen from Korea awaiting your sixth
open-heart surgery in green garden's affectionate arms and
returning this touch by touching red velvet Austen Rose
petals while beholding "Earth's Children," the sculpture of
hands and feet held around the globe and knowing that your
two best friends in Seoul are holding your hands and feet.

Or imagine being a widow confined yet buoyed by lazuli-
blue-bright sky erasing four walls to set sail with Chagal's
dream of floating up, up, up into the cosmos of your
wedding day with your lost, now found beloved—pausing
on Beethoven's island of trembling Spring's Sonata Number
Five and forgetting completely the tatters of your torn life.
Or imagine the sculpted Rodin-like Asclepius whose
Polaris-arms surrender to uplifting you above desires and
loathings to behold true cosmic north—home—
homeostasis—hospitality—front-line of health, liberty,
happiness, all besting the sapphire-hot joy of distant Icarus
(once reliant upon Daedalus-wax-and-feather wings) now
dancing joy's frenzy, not to forget how fragile we all are,
but to remember our strength—our wise and medicinal
innocence and our calling to make of our hearts a home to
have and to hold, to liberate and to love what shines through
all the bodies that cannot last.

M. Ann Reed

What says the Earth?
Druid Circle, Aberystwyth

The Earth guides a visitor in the following words.

Fresh lavender. Fragments. Secrets
more than forty-five thousand years old like
the Tao in the hand, the sun leafing out.

Within Druid Tower, childhood's cool, dark
wishing well. Stars seem to drown. Yet climb
the winding stairs—look up! They live through
the cross-shaped, always-open window—thin place
where air and stone kiss to birth the space between.

Is the other world inside or out? Or both?
Out from your heart Logos and Eros arms
meet above Druid Circle's standing stones
to marry azure sky with viridian sea,
their center marking the ebony rock
rising from sea's heartbeat, accepting
crashing waves—breaking them—turning brine
          to Pegasus-wings.

There—above and below at heart's center,
you are Celtic tree of life, half burning
from its roots to its tip, half green with leaves—
harvesting and planting—both meeting
at one time. Each "letting-go" a receiving,
a new life—blessed and bewildered.

M. Ann Reed

The Walls Cried[58]

Three hundred heads
  bent in prayer,
Three hundred breaths
  as one;
Three hundred heartbeats
  beating—
   Mothers, daughters,
   Fathers, sons.

Each wish a vibration,
  Each echo a chant,
   Raised upward and outward,
    They together incant.

In young voices and old,
  Stories are told,
   Lives unfold, as
    Their futures take hold.

Within the walls that house these persons,
  The walls that hear their prayers,
The walls inadvertently made prison—
  Now contain their tears.

Voices sharing prayers
Were now voices joined in terror;
  Where are all the heartbeats going,
Absorbed in maleficent error…

And all around, as people died,
The walls slumped their shoulders,
  …and cried.

Vinni Relwani

Change[59]

The present moment
is long and empty
Tom Waits's music aside
his voice
reminds me of sandpaper
and a flower too
but I don't remember its name.
He will keep me company
until dawn
if dawn will wait for me.
It is hard to concentrate
on the present moment
if in vain a vague future
insists to tease me
and a past now opaque and late.
Tom's voice reminds me
of three packs of cigarettes
if it was a plant
it would be a cardoon;
surely he drinks
rust-honey-tar infusions.
I must not lose the rhythm
I can't
change is close
and dawn is close too
I imagine it
mandarin-lemon
striped with mallow leaves.

Angelo Rizzi

No man's land

Three o'clock resonates
I feel as if I am
in an endless land
I travel
from one night shore
to the other
inside
a black and white world.
Soft trumpet sounds
percussion
the night as a spider
spins his song
and catches
voiceless insects, sublime notes
and reflection
when it becomes rumination.
Night says
and the spider says too
that humility is today
a weakness.
I listen to sleeping trees
and mute creatures
and finally
my thoughts are silent.
So peaceful!
I feel I am
in a no man's land.

Angelo Rizzi

A Confession of Appetite[60]

Break the nest I'm told the best meat is tender.
When cucumber dried in the sun I begged
for breakfast
and at home nudged
the lip of a ceramic bowl.
Kissing it was salvation because
I could eat tender meat then.
And rinsed clean,
look into my mother's mirror.

Now, I feed the dogs by handfuls—
biscuits in bone shapes and waxed beef
that I taste first.
My son eats candy daily; it sticks to
the tip of his nose in brown-gum smiles until
his teacher asks
"Why every day?"

I'm tender meat, I think in a broken nest
trying to piece the shell back again.

Aparna Upadhyaya Sanyal

Early Larger-than-Life Memories[61]

Grandma carried away butter dabs
in her large Burberry duffel
and hard rolls in the folds of
her Dior trench,
under which she wore, like
the mark of penance,
crumpled pale cotton sarees
with a white blouse always
stained at the neck,
as if to say it did not care.
She pulled out knots from white
uncombed hair in front of
other passengers, and ate the free
apples, although she had
all 36 teeth removed young,
and altogether,
"for exigency" she always said.
She ate, at home, large bites of
fruit—
melons, mangoes, papaya—
nothing escaped her steel jaws
that looked new-born in
certain types of light.
She stored sachets of Sweet & Low
until her cupboards overflowed,
alongside pashminas and
shah-toosh shawls so soft,
they flowed
like moon-chilled water over our
grandfather on cold nights.
Once,
he poked a hole through one
with the tip of his big toenail,
the precious weave broken;
at once his man-help
cat-stepped from the shadows
to pounce on it with a clipper.
There it sat,

that pleasure-seeking nail,
nibbed with endangered fur,
half-moon flaking, clot-smiling with guilt
at us grandchildren called in
to witness its culling;
a cautionary tale against
reaching up unthinking to pleasures
untrammelled.

Grandma
walked alongside grandfather.
"Nani" she, but *"Nana-ji"* him;
the *"ji"* being the respect he gave
back.
Honorific they, them both;
in my dreams he wakes refreshed
and her eyes hollow out.
Nearby, violence and the sound
of her prayer-beads.
He, bead-sweating,
ittar broiling at temples,
for her, no other words but
snow like sugar and
death-cold.
Together, they fed peacocks in
the winter sun.
Never side by side, but
she, in wide arcs of grain,
flung every 4pm exactly,
over a feral garden and
he, in wet flourishes of Urdu;
Ghalib and Mir Taqi Mir dripping pink
Campari diamond drops,
intumescing
down the side of a crystal glass.
Always people called her
his mother,
and women flirted, not knowing
how close they came to truth, and
almost guessing the distance

between their beds or even their rooms.
Their giggles grated her nerves
but she knew that
he was Power;
which was to say he would bring her
trench coats and handbags
from foreign lands
to hide her decay.
And which was to say,
he would allow her games
played from a crippled bedside
for the dregs of their together life.

And she would let him smile, but
only in the brief sunlight
outside the sweltering heirloom
that was
their together home.

Aparna Upadhyaya Sanyal

Grouted into Those Tiles[62]

I see people in the patterned tiles; a lion howling in orange
grout.
Stick men eat a Jack Sprat lunch and old water covers it all.

I tell myself stories in this shower, workshopping tales past
dungeon and dragon paths. Triumph at last.

I am used to alone; to the lushness of silence and
the untold trivia of living out a life.

And then, you turn to me with your eyes and your grasp,
as if to say, 'Never leave this place' and for that second, I do
not.

Wet notes sound inside of the pillow,
I have scribbled them there in screams and sometimes-sobs.

It knows I'm lonely when the lights are too bright:
this tile wall in the bathroom stall.

Stupid-stupid-stupid mocking nightstand,
fool girl running away for a wish in a greedy mirror.

I have sat a crown on your head—not seen the
purpled bruises below. My Golgotha is at your feet.

Now I'm sat in a speeding car, blade consigned to mocking
highway. My eviscerated eyes are dry at last.

Aparna Upadhyaya Sanyal

Whispering the Family Tree to my Son at Night[63]

Let me tell you
the inside-vein secrets of our kin.

Here on the soft yellow of my wrist
lies the heartbeat of my ancestors:
the rabbit I show you to keep wolves at bay.
There on your scalp unwrinkled,
are the worries your grandfather does not show
and the wonder of his curious gaze.
Let me tell you of your grandmother:
she, who picks apart the seams that hold tension and
ignites the wreckage with her nails.
She, who pours proud loud water at digression
and eats hearts for a meal.
On her side, uncles purple with rage,
ripening in the sun with a soft leather smell.

Daadi has walked the roof, the yard, the house:
the tiny circuits ascribing life and sanity.
Like tubers bursting red in confused self-awareness,
her garden grows still.
Par-Daadi once ate the sun inside the house;
no frills or giggles. Unadorned.
"*Nahi*" was a giant "no" sutured to her back.
She is my unmet mirror, gone too soon.
But, not before I have swallowed the razors
from her mouth.

And here then, is my ever-after concern:
the flowing of this stardust from me to you.
So, if this whispering can staunch the flow
of this blood between us,
I will curl into you each night and do it anew.

And I will tell you then, of *Par-Naani*:
she, who comes at night and feeds you grapes
twice-chewed from her mouth.
But, this is not her haunting, it is her consecration.
For she is saying, "*Know your angels, child.*

But know your demons too."
We may be code-named for our sins by our elders,
grouted into the shell of everyday,
but *you* are named for our eyes forever—
when they had not seen madness yet.

Sleep child, for you know this now.
And the weather inside your home is a storm no more.

Aparna Upadhyaya Sanyal

"Words Joyously" to "Left Behind"

I
Words joyously
offer-make a plastic
medium, where the
chaos-mind re-
minds the solid earth
of its liquidity,
thin air
of its capacity
creative, where the
body-chemical re-
aches the play-ground,
tongues the ebru-esque floor,
sucks its teeth into the sweet breasts of re-
presentation,
at the bud
of the skies,
enreasoned-dream
sets up the tent and the
camp fire.

II
Twisting woods, Molding stones
Singing the odes carries the loads, for
All work and no play maketh
The once lovely Jack, a serious, dull boy.

III
no matter Us,
Animaty keeps rolling.
no matter Jack,
Plastic, chaotic, liquid, holding a playful grin
Animaty
Keeps
Rolling.

LEFT BEHIND

Halil Suat Saraç

Bending into Blue[64]

Caught in cabin-dreams
I rest my head
in branches of living green

in a mystery of blue
in the miracle of morning
lighting windows
where I slept
where dreams entered
unannounced

waking I put aside
unborn issues
waiting in secret places
my mind unfettered
I rise into this day

questing—in meditation—
without thought
with branches hovering like
wings of some better angels
a presence held in dawn-light
like butterflies

with living movement
between the leaves—green singing
that calls my name.

Allegra Jostad Silberstein

The Flowing[65]

In the shadow of a dream
rising in the night
lotus lilies invade the water
white petals around a golden center.

In the somewhere between
found in folds of inner sight
reflections of trees
grace the rippling stream.

In the place where things dwell
architecture of the moment
thought transports into
waves of hills and valleys.

In the ghazal of folded hours
whispered into the void
water sound of a fountain
the music flowing over.

Allegra Jostad Silberstein

Plastic promise[66]

Pretty petals float through my dreams,
their iridescence
perfumed with ambergris and starlight,
a heady mix of the faintly impossible.

I don't complain, dreams are such cohesive intangibles
that truth is everywhere, yet nowhere at all.

I am accustomed, now, to the liquidity of thought
that speaks to my soul,
bypassing logic and all my natural censorship.

Perhaps our minds are elastic at night,
when the wind
wends its way into dreams,
changing from gushing air to rushing tides,
from undulating waves to the
splish-splash of rain upon roots,
germinating fronds in a flash of rustling questions….

In dreams, my questing is heeded,
transmuted to colours in simple strands.

They ebb and flow, tangle and twist, searching, seeking—
rightly or randomly—
some form of impalpable answer.

Enlightenment softly skims the oblivion that is me,
the dream-dipped sleeper.

When I wake, it is all just a wisp of truthful elusiveness.

If I am lucky, I am marked in daylight by the stains of
veracity
that linger in places I never reach, but define who I become.

Now I am awake, the cloak of sense that has drifted
across my shifting dreams is wholly cast off.

I become aware of the *non*-sense of it all.

I have learnt, though, not to tug at seams, hoping for
enlightenment.
If I do, I risk ripping the fabric and unmasking not
understanding, or solace,
but something sinister in its sterility.

At worst, nightmares, in unspoken shades of woven fears.
At best—neutrality.

By daylight, the dream cloaks shift to nothing more
than the moulded shawls of
plastic promise.

Hayley Ann Solomon

The Butterfly Effect[67]

I heard the wings of butterfly
on a day soft-still with heat,
when my heart was wholly open,
and my soul in soul's retreat.

So soft the sound, so simple, soft and sweet, I swear I heard
it shimmer—
though sound and light don't meet.

Yet the simple hush of butterfly, all a-tremble in still air,
caused rushing rains in Jinzhou-high thermal winds to
flair…

The smallest act has consequence—
trajectories change with thought,
and plastic
sipped, or ripped or torn or shipped
brings death—
a lingering death hard-wrought.

Wrappings, laminates, careless bags and straws
are the flapping wings of butterfly,
in the universe of laws.

Ah, immortal gods of plastic, created by your serfs,
We knew not what we did
when we brought you forth to earth.
Worthless, you serve us once then laugh.
We bin, we bury—abandon you—
then full incur your wrath.

With a butterfly flutter we made you immortal—
now, you refuse to die
and the storm is coming.

Fish squirm, you choke them with your spite. In nets and
seas and fins and throats the world… *our* world… has no
respite.

We have set our trajectory and unless we are open to
alternatives,
mitigate our mistakes,

We will die and you will be eternal,
Oh plastic gods,
on thrones of Junk
piled high.

Hayley Ann Solomon

Whose fault is that?[68]

Synthetic trinkets on a shelf have a half life
of pleasure and an eternity of doom.

Plastic mugs outlive their laughs,
but continue to exist—
rude slogans
of memory.

Artificial plants
blossom fronds of dust,
fading with generations of neglect.

Plastic
is not permitted the grace of oblivion—
discarded,
it begs
to biodegrade,
but is denied
the dignity.

So it transitions to
deadly drifter,
throttling and choking
in passive
impassivity.

Its legacy is not the usefulness it was,
But the evil it has become.

Whose fault is that?

Hayley Ann Solomon

Prayer[69]
(*an acrostic*)

Please, if you can hear me,
Reach out to my loved ones in your realm.
Assure them I still love them.
Young at heart, I still think about them,
Every day, every night, every season,
Remember that we'll someday be together.

Abbie Taylor

A Plastic Made Treasure[70]

I wanted a sturdy doll.
Not the one made of old cloths!
I wanted to run with my doll
and not to keep her still
and sleepy on a sofa.
The little princess playing
with her bisque doll
was always told
to be gentle with her
to make her look
like a real little lady

Now with my plastic doll
I am the happiest of girls
running and running
holding my darling
while in the winds
my curls are dancing

I would not change my doll
for any other toy
not even for the story book
holding my dreams of future joy

Plastic, bisque, or cloth
Plastic most resembles me
The doll who makes me flee
to the castle of my dreams
where I and my doll are both queens

Luisa Ternau

A Time of Life[71]

Drop by drop
We are being emptied
Slowly slowly
Not to disturb our neighbours
Sad is not our destination
Sad is this time when
The sunlight is out
And we are indoors
Windows closed
The room artificially filled with
Air, forced upon us
To fix us in aging time
Drop by drop
There is an end
To the medicine bottle, too.
Its odour will linger
For a while, then even
The memory will
Fade, unexplained
Unexplainable, perhaps

By then
Nobody will care
Or even know
When a happier time
Was ours
Only …
This life can
Nourish us with
Such beautiful dreams
We all fall for
With an open heart

Luisa Ternau

Out of Their Cage[72]

Quivering lights
waiting for the night
to bloom
budding dreams of birds
just released from their cage
The stars have not come yet
Some clouds are lingering
in their luminous direction
The birds in fear of darkness
are hopping back inside
At dawn every door
will be ready to snap.
The victims will still be asleep
dreaming a dance treading
on the clouds, their thoughts still looking
for the unborn stars.

Luisa Ternau

Seaside Lullaby[73]

Lingering by the shore tonight
I know
The waves sing you a lullaby
Little child of the sea
While the horizon disappears
In the longing that will not
Be put to sleep. Neither by moonshine
Will your sweet smile reveal itself
Nor by the dazzling glare of the sun
When the light burns all memories
Of past laughter.
In your azure joy
You will not wake
You will hide in the waves
In the long waves of the Ocean
Moving backward and forward
In forever times
Not caring about past, present or future,
Rejoicing only in the soothing sound
Surrounding your dreams,
Little child, little dream of the waves.

Luisa Ternau

The Voice[74]

Looking up;
The moon swallowed
By skyscrapers,
A voice whispers, sings softly,
Life runs in the winds,
Rushing around corners,
Airing everything
With gigantic draughts.
Millennia will pass by
And this voice will be heard out here
By the mind of
Someone who will be around,
Letting the winds
Rush through the windows;
Yet nothing will be known
About this life of so long ago,
Spring after spring
Blooming
Autumn after autumn,
Preparing to generate again.
Only this voice will remain,
Echoing in the chasms
Of time.

Luisa Ternau

Summer Sunday Morning[75]

It is nearly summer's dawn
as we stroll the canopied street
in the diffuse magical morning
light.

Single notes from a piano
are being slowly
played

Each note drifting
on the already warm air
upwards towards the trees;
a humid hymn for a still sleeping
neighbourhood.

Eventually, I recognize it as Bach
being played at
a very slow
tempo.

The notes are correct
but keyed as if someone is practicing,
learning the movement
in the summer's early
silence.

The music wafts as we walk,
the sun at our backs
projects our long shadows
as the melody teaches us
enjoyment.

Edward Tiesse

The Mask-Maker's Bian Lian[76]

In the by-lanes of the old city
Where life lives in labyrinths,
Dwells the old, old mask-maker
With a flowing beard,
His face, a pattern of wrinkles.
His eyes bear a distant gleam of years gone by,
Of love and yearning, of loss and pain, of wisdom and calm.

He sits in the bazaar corner selling masks that smile and
masks that cry,
Masks that are asleep and masks that are awake,
Masks of kings and masks of paupers,
Those of love and of hate.
Passers-by stop to pick up the ones they like,
Some buy, some haggle, some just go—
The old man looks on.

He knows this game has been like this always—
Each morning he displays his wares
Each night he counts and keeps them safe.
He knows people get weary, he knows people love change.
So he designs masks of demons and devils,
Of clowns and buffoons, of saints and philosophers,
And smiles, for he knows it all.

The mask-maker's fame spreads across the land
And reaches the king, who sends his soldiers at once
To have him summoned to the royal court,
"I want a mask that is unique, the best you have ever made.
Make it in three days or have yourself hanged," he
thundered.
"Yes, sire," answered the old man.
Turning around, he smiled, for he knew it all.

At night he lit a fire, and sat to shape a mask that would
immortalize him.
He yearned to create a masterpiece, a right concoction of
ingredients
Blended with the most beautiful hues,

A mask
that would be the epitome of creation.
The light of the fire glistened in his eyes, his heart was
ablaze
A song rose from the depths of his soul
The chaos in it was quelled.

He worked night after night, pouring his art into his act of
creating
A mask that would exemplify his craftsmanship
Till he shaped the mask of a Human!
Into it he poured compassion and peace,
Love and bliss, wisdom and knowledge.
Came the king's men on the third day and he marched with
them.
His heart quivering with joy for he knew that all he knew
had shaped the mask.

The king, on seeing the mask mocked, "This ain't no grand
thing."
"My lordship", said the mask-maker, "wearing it
Will change the world and the world will change for you.
The glory of this mask will bring treasures at your feet
Yet you will have no need of them—
For you will know peace and love and desire knowledge
And know no ambition or greed or lust."

The king did so and was dumbfounded,
He wept with the joy of seeing it all.
"O mask-maker", he said, "Your wisdom is profound, your
creation priceless.
I shall make the mask my own face,
So that I can proclaim to the world
That it's better to be HUMAN rather than be a king."
The old man sighed and smiled yet again, for he knew it all!

Deepa Vanjani

From the Scent of Trees[77]

A hawk with wings extended
flew over Enoch.

The prophet's eyes had dimmed
two decades earlier,

and so, like a time traveler,
the bird remained invisible.

As usual, the soothsayer spoke
to himself,
effusive over his latest revelations,

casting them like stones
from a ridge-top

at unbelievers, harlots
and flightless angels.

God Himself rejoiced
that his disciple refrained
from condemning the small souls
of dogs, of goats, of doves,
of orphaned children.

Enoch chronicled his usual obsessions:

* the sun setting into a sea of fire,
* celestial giants who mate with dreaming women,
* a void absent of stars and planets,
* imaginary seraphim to answer his continuous questions,
* a list of curses and lamentations,
* founts of never-ending light,
* confluences of clouds, winds and water,
* hidden oases and bottomless ravines,
* multi-coloured hillsides of exotic jewels,
* internments and the Final Judgement.

What could the villagers do for such a man
whose brain had shed years ago
like snakeskin in the desert?

(He had already gone deaf
from the shouting of his own voice.)

Still, he drew the curious
and their unleavened offerings:

tongues craved his red-wine vinegar
if, for nothing else,
its bitter authenticity.

At dusk, an angel manifested itself:

it roughed up bay leaves,
pine needles, wormwood, sage
and buck brush in its palms,

held out its hands
filled with the ethereal potpourri
under the old oracle's nose.

Though the wanderer
couldn't see the offering,
the spirit-being communed with him.

The supernatural are by nature discrete,
and though they can cross over
from a mirror universe,

they do their best
to dart out of the way
from the peripheral vision
of pilgrims.

(Thus their affection
for the deaf and blind
who allow them to loiter
with impunity.)

Like most mortals
who have lost everything,

Enoch was at his sanest
when his raw mind reminded him
to abandon his thoughts.

Even saints from time to time
need to bow
like horses at a river

and slake
from the scent of trees.

Peter Verbica

Chase

We went to Morecambe to chase the sunset;
Along the way, many happy dogs
ran on the beach after low tide:
Pug, Lowchen, Dalmatian, Mutt;
Several horses wandered leisurely in a natural reserve.

An empty stomach led us to the Royal Heysham;
With satisfaction and glasses of the strongest ale,
we continued the march.

A play of colours was right on show in the sky:
Three arrows of light blue clouds
Turned into pink, orange, then gold,
Stretching out to the horizon in one,
Leaving the moon behind.
Then was night.

More can be
Tomorrow

Anson Wang

Dream

I have a dream
I want to see more than the soles of others

You came bringing fears and worries in to town
And joy only to me

I danced in the sky
Overlooking those who trod on me

I saw the sea so near
My view was blocked for so long

I heard the whistle of wind turning into roars
Blowing away everything on the way

I love showers from the sky
Killing the itchiness from the sun

I kept my eyes wide open
Before you disappeared as the opportunity was rare

Anson Wang

Maybe

The noon started with an unexpected call
Maybe an expected call

He paid his final visit.
Reaching out his hand,
He said gently, "It's time maybe".
"Please come with me".

He whispered in your ears.
You shall be free,
Through the kisses of the fire,
From the flesh and bones,
From the worries and cares.

Maybe thirty minutes,
Maybe more,
You shall know in their tears.
Though you can no longer see or hear.
You shall know on your path.

You will be buried in their world.
And they in yours.

From now on,
Just you and me.
Maybe.

Anson Wang

None to None

None
Hundreds of drops
Tadpoles swimming happily
Disappeared in the angry waterfalls

Two broken green leaves
Leeches resting leisurely
Swallowed by the calm winds
None

Anson Wang

Three Goldfishes

Three goldfishes walked to the sea
to lie down in a hole unknown

Three goldfishes lay down in the hole unknown
to feel tears of the sea unbound

Three goldfishes felt tears of the sea unbound
to flood in the hole unaware

The sea saw three goldfishes come near,
swallowing them in finding a cure.

Anson Wang

Condado and the Sea

There is a little bit of brown beneath the blue
the crashing foam as waves lick rocks
like the top of an ice cream, melting
always melting, yet never humid to the tongue.

It is overcast today, but the tint on the horizon
says something better, the family 5 floors
down is studious in their life-sized chess
of black and white squares standing fast against
remembrance of the largest hurricane in 100 years
the taxi driver said, her New York slang shifting
to Nuevo Rican as smoothly as piña colada past the hard
architecture of teeth, to find the velvet in a swallow
of lush, black player losing 4 pieces to white's
5 and the why of the sun seen peeking past layers
of grey is shed in light and darker skin like the tanned
rocks with a little lizard moss every now and then
as a measure of success.

The loneliest sentry knew the allure of his lady and rum
and leaving nothing but clothes and musket to guard
the seaways and the roar of waves enough to drive the crazy
from him, soft brown flesh singing songs with Caribbean
drums and the tapas of skin leaving little but dry mouth
longing for more and it is never too hot here and the heat
of close breath is just a soft whisper in an ear and thus the
devil's lookout appeared in history and others shrank from
its languid tones but not the unnamed watcher, his home
somewhere where iguanas tread and stare and wait for
the space between the tradewinds to send another ship
and another till they all are sunk from the cannon fire
pounding their sides and leaving iron balls skipping waves
like pebbles on a pond, like little boys in the discovery of
all that goes on between the cover of day before it peels
another layer and darkness.

Is there a lull in these ever-present winds, is there a place
where the sun won't compete with tomorrow and
the face of it like sundials in sunsets or shadows

on the chess board and checkmates of a thousand ages
and ever-present planes flying in and out and over but
never under the waves until they're lost for good and unable
to recover. Is there a stop to all the banged-up buildings
basted
by the hurricane's love and now waiting for money
to drop from some heaven-blue sky to be restored, or the
little man
with the cane who offers his advice and hopes for maybe
dinner and a life filled with more than just tomorrow
like yesterday and onward forever.

Or is it only that waves will speak the final words and
the graves of yesterday will be lost inside the jungle
and the lonely sentry is now just forgotten sorrows
and the sweat of a life lived in brown flesh beneath
blue and white caps and every change of venue
merely another story that never really ends?

Bruce Arlen Wasserman

Anagnorisis[78]

Inside the living room the dog's hackles
run along his back, nose spoiling windows
cleaned yesterday. Cold drafts growl.
Grinning door-frame cracks. A distant door slams.

New Year chimes in with cracked bells and the lights
flicker then go out. The heat pump shudders
to a stop. The dog noses the stained glass
then snuffles for the lead behind the door.

On the walk by the river edged with ice,
trying not to, I can still catch a word
or a phrase, something you would have said
in your foggy, puffed-out breathless tone.

Staring at the brown, meandering length,
you said, "All way to the coast: next stop
Antarctica. Imagine that!" Then you
left with the arrival of fresh spring rain.

Like the dog's, my bladder's full, noses running.
Long pink sympathetic tongue. Anxious glance.
Home territory calls, already marked,
so distant frozen wastes will have to wait.

George Watt

By a river in Zhejiang Province
pondering the end of the world[79]

Wyndham's Triffids might bring it about,
Young McQueen's The Blob.
McCarthy? Under-the-bed-reds,
and for Stalin, Nazis: Nazis, Stalin.

Or St John's big bang will end it all—
sleepy heads popping up from open graves
for the final judgement that will damn
well prove Richard Dawkins wrong.

But on this river's burnt orange scum
an endless procession floats by
of cups, boxes, crates, packing for all must-haves.
The turbulent brown waters dwarf a little man

agog in the mad-dog mid-day sun,
squid-oil dripping on a sweaty shirt.
On! On! On! to the broad Pacific
the sweeping detritus cries, harbingers

of our imminent, oncoming end
by polyclonal, polydipsic, polystyrene foam—
something doomsday prophets, ancient
and modern, couldn't begin to dream of.

George Watt

Desire in Winter: in memoriam

Conjure a sheet of ice,
razor thin, crystal clear.
Peer through air-bubbled runnels
at a clean but distorted world.

A flighty task: snatch
a fistful of gale-blown cloud,
weigh-up its weightless grey, or

visit a bear in hibernation,
feel her barely breathing,
Darwin-dormant in her long sleep.

So too earthbound seeds
inert yet dreaming of
netted dragonfly wings and
the golden pollen puffs at sunset.

Pretending thus to toy
with Winter's wiles
this sad, phony Orpheus
in dark-walled tunnels seeks your eye,

peering through blocks of blue ice.
Listens for strains of your voice
somewhere in a vast lucent cavern,
crystal strung.

But a bendy bus belts me with mud.
The leaf-laced wind whirls and snaps
like a villain in an old cloak.

In this arctic presence
my ardent desire for Winter's heart
thaws into wants for a warm bath
and a fresh face.

George Watt

Eagle-Owl in a Yunan Chophouse[80]

Fashioned for hunger and the kill: now caged.
Conscious of eye unlike her tanked neighbours:
eels, catfish, blue crabs with grand pincers tied—
all swoopable things in another life.
Six feet of wing reduced to nervous ticks.
Rats dropped at talons stained with her own shit.
In the steamy air and eaters' babble
a worthy patron bids. Imagines her
roasting on a spit, later to declaim
with the wise ancients, "You are what you eat."

But (chef's eyes to the heavens) a *gweilo*
outbids him for this rare avian fare,
and claims the puzzled creature as his own.
"*Yangguizi!*" yells the defeated, banging
the door wildly on exit. The driver
too shakes his rattled head: a savage bird
in a cage in his car. Life's a struggle!
And drive to the countryside! Anywhere.
Now freed from cage, tapes and hood, she hisses.
Mortiferous talons press on red earth

again, and again, eyeing her saviours
with razored implacable hate. Of flight
or revenge she chooses to go: labours,
then lifts and lifts, the envy of angels.
A warm, unsettled breeze blows across neat,
odiferous fields. Bleeding staunched, they sit
on a grubby blanket to face their lunch:
damp crackers, wilting greens, tired tomato.
Grinning at a now empty container
one quips, "You are what you eat!"

George Watt

Plastic[81]

The great God of death no longer draws his sword,
looses an arrow, disperses black plagues.

Instead, his minions collect pale, thin substances,
discarded by careless hands.

They drop his new weapons into the seas and water ways;
he watches them being swallowed.

Life after life is extinguished by one deadly piece,
surviving each killing unscathed.

A seagull chokes and dies—the soft weapon re-emerging
after the flesh has disintegrated.

Along its trajectory the *weapon* passes through
a turtle, pelican, dolphin, young whale.

The great God of death watches in contented silence,
grinning, he is walking on easy street.

Mocco Wollert

Plastic Nonet[82]

Hands
printed
body parts
powder flowing
printer starting up
re-creating lost limbs
coloured pink like living flesh
torsos stacked high on hidden shelves
robots wait silently in deep vaults

Mocco Wollert

Declaration of Plastic[83]

The combo of phenol and formaldehyde,
I was born in nineteen and seven.
The older I become, the harder humans can turn the tide
As I'm getting more and more invincible and unbroken.

My omnipresence even impresses myself
Since you can hardly name a place where I'm not found.
I'm a gigantic monster grown from a little elf.
Your indulgence enables me to keep gaining ground.

Every niche is piled with my non degradable waste,
Seas choked with my own kind.
Even giant whales swallow tonnes of my rubbish in haste.
Marine creatures' guts full of my particles is a real find.

Once the Earth was mostly blue and green,
A wondrously beautiful planet
With the most precious clear air and natural sheen,
The loveliest sunrise and sunset.

It's turning pale, sick and brown because of me.
My rampant growth will continue
Until I conquer the whole world and thee.
The only way to stop me is the unity of you and you and
every you!

But I'm sure you're not determined to abandon me!
Embrace me until death! Ha! Ha! Ha!
Free, free, free! I'm free!
And you? Bah! Humbug! Bah! Bah! Bah!

Maggie Wong

True Grit: I'm Plastic[84]

They call me cheap, taking me for granted.
"Environmentally bad", they've often ranted.
I've been around for a century, that's true.
Yet, my value to them, some don't have a clue.
I'm versatile, malleable, pliable and synthetic,
Studied at the university and polytechnic;
Found in factories, packaging, bags and toys,
Daily used by men, women, girls and boys.
Beaten, stretched, melted and molded,
I come in all shapes and sizes, flat or folded.
With true grit, I serve many a need,
Bearing the brunt of people's greed,
Not easily snuffed out by piteous platitude,
Wanton abuses or demeaning attitude.
I am true to myself, as it is only right to be:
I am true grit! I'm plastic of unique quality!

Libby Wong

She visits from New Zealand[85]

We stand together on the sand.
A desert diamond in the palm of her hand.
In Riyadh I give it to Imthyiaz. Say, *a plain silver*
setting. Simple chain. It's for my daughter.

At Al Ula we climb an ancient citadel.
Walk narrow streets. Mud brick homes
all empty. Small souk, silent. Ahmed says
the village is a National Heritage site.
They moved everyone into crisp new
housing blocks. His mother lived here.
She had friends. Her children were born here.
Now when she visits she cries.

Beyond Al Ula they once pitched goat-hair tents.
We fly Air Saudia, a thousand kilometres
from home. Drive through desert to reach
stone-hewn tombs. Al-Hijir Archeological Site.
موقع الهجر الأثري. مدائن صالح Madain Saleh.
Tomb of the Maiden. A Persian rose above a doorway.
Look, I say to my daughter, *the face of Medusa.*
And see these stepped pediments above us.
From the Assyrians. Pathways to heaven.
I photograph the dark opening of a small tomb
half-hidden behind a gnarled acacia. Ahmed
points to Aramaic letters: Built in the reign of
King Aretas who loved his people. 31 AD. Inside
we place our hands over ancient chisel marks.
Cold stone. Narrow recesses along walls
where once dead were laid. We pitch
tents. Sit on scattered carpets.
Wait for darkness.

Marjory Woodfield

THE POETS
Brief Biographies based on texts provided by the Poets

JOY AL-SOFI is a published writer of poetry, fiction and nonfiction. She was a winner in the International Proverse Poetry Prize inaugural year. She has an MFA in Creative Writing and has been teaching English in Hong Kong since 2004. Originally from the USA, and formerly a lawyer, her recent interests include videoing African wildlife.

SOLOMON AU YEUNG was selected as one of the Teen Poets in the 34th National Poetry Summit organized by the China Poetry Journal. Because of this, Solomon's first full book-length manuscript was published by a Beijing independent book house, known as a Cycle of Self: Beginning to End. Solomon has based his English writings on his life and upbringing in Hong Kong to come up with a mini-scale chapbook in the form of a Japanese Origami Project.

Solomon has received, to date, the following awards and recognitions.

For Chinese poetry, a grouped verse entry was selected as a 2nd-runner-up in The 16th National Literature Community of DaiLei's Short Prose & Poetry Contest Top Prize. The online entry of his work, 'Raging Blood', in one of the biggest Chinese Poetry-writing groups was selected as one of 51 finalists for the Taiwan TaiKe 6-verse Poetry Prize. Another piece, 'Coloured Fish', was nominated for the 2019 HaiLing National Modern Poetry Contest and has passed through the preliminary stage to receive a first-phase Selection Prize.

For English poetry, Solomon was a runner-up for the inaugural International Woolf Poetry Prize with his piece, 'The Cycle of Life'. His poem, 'Snapshots by Heart', was shortlisted for the Proverse International Poetry Award. 'Flirt with the Unknown' was shortlisted in the 2018 Momaya Poetry Competition. His work about freedom, 'Flying Kite', received an honourable mention as a semi-finalist in the 5th Annual Songs of Eretz Poetry Award Contest. For his shorter piece, 'Mr. Perfectionist…Mr.

Monet', he was long-listed in the Cornwall Contemporary Poetry Festival Open Poetry Competition.

Much of the poetic material is drawn from his imagination and observation in his birthplace, Hong Kong.

SUI PING AU YEUNG is a poet and poetry translator. Her poetry has appeared in several magazines like *Voice & Verse Poetry Magazine*, *Off the Roll*, *Poetry+* and *Qiu Ying Shi Kan*. Between 2012 and 2017, she was one of the editors of *Voice & Verse Poetry Magazine*.

REEMA BANIABBASI was born in Dubai, United Arab Emirates and lived in Boston, MA, USA from 2008 to 2018 before returning to her hometown with degrees in psychology and counseling psychology. As an emerging writer, she has published poems in *Beautiful Minds UAE*, *Art Ascent*, and *Snapdragon* and articles in *Womankind Magazine* and in newsletters affiliated with the American Psychological Association.

THEA BIESHEUVEL is a prolific writer and teacher of both short stories and poetry. She was the runner-up in the 2018 International Proverse Poetry Prize competition. Her forte is an "outsider" view of Australian life and culture, having migrated to that country from her birth country, the Netherlands. She has published three anthologies and a short memoir about her antecedents, *Dutch Treat*.

LIAM BLACKFORD is an Australian lawyer living and working in Hong Kong.

MARÍA ELENA BLANCO. Poet, essayist and translator born in Havana, Cuba, who writes predominantly in her native Spanish. Having spent a good part of her formative years in New York, she translates her own poetry into English and has also developed her own English poetic voice in a style quite distinguishable from her Spanish one.

She holds degrees in French, Spanish and Latin American literatures. After an initial period of teaching, since 1986 she has worked for the United Nations successively as translator, reviser and chief of translation section and is now on the UN freelance translators' roster.

Her published work includes poetry collections Posesión por pérdida (Sevilla: Barro, 1990; Santiago de Chile: Libra, 1990), Corazón sobre la tierra / tierra en los Ojos (Matanzas, Cuba: Vigía, 1998), Alquímica memoria (Madrid: Betania, 2001), Mitologuías (Madrid: Betania, 2001), Vestal Myths/Solstice Fires (Vienna: Labyrinth, 2001), Felix Austria/Reality Fireworks (Vienna: Labyrinth, 2004), danubiomediterráneo /mittelmeerdonau (Vienna: Labyrinth, 2005, Spanish-German), Wilde Lohe (Klagenfurt/Celovec: Wieser, 2007, in German translation), El amor incontable (Madrid: Vitrubio, 2008); Havanity / Habanidad (Miami, U.S.A.: Baquiana, 2010, English-Spanish poetry anthology), Escrito en lenguas (Santiago, Chile; Verbodesnudo, 2015); Sobresalto al vacío (Santiago, Chile: Mago Eds., 2015); Botín. Antología personal (Leiden, Netherlands: Bokeh, 2016); Oro vano (Santiago, Chile: Verbodesnudo, 2019); as well as a book of literary criticism, Asedios al texto literario (Madrid: Betania, 1999), and a volume of critical essays on Cuba, Devoraciones. Ensayos de período especial (Leiden, Netherlands: Almenara, 2016). She has also published Spanish translations of several Austrian poets, including M-T. Kerschbaumer and Gerhard Kofler, among others.

She is a frequent participant in international poetry festivals and literary colloquia. She won the Grand Prix International de Poésie of the Académie Orient-Occident (Rumania) in 2016 and was a prize-winner in each of the Proverse Poetry Prize competitions from 2016 to 2019 inclusive. She divides her time between her home in Vienna (Austria) and regular trips to Chile and Spain.

RAYMOND CALBAY is the founder of PageJump Media. He has degrees in literature and communication from the University of Santo Tomas, where he also attended its 10th National Writers Workshop. His poetry and creative nonfiction have appeared in *Yellow Medicine Review* and *Ani Literary Yearbook*, among others. His poems have received honorable mentions from contests organised by

Meritage Press and also by the Japan Information and Cultural Center.

PAOLA CARONNI hails from Italy and has been living in Asia since 1995. She resides now in Hong Kong, where she works as a translator and tutor of Italian language. She holds an MFA in Creative Writing from the University of Hong Kong and an MA in English Language and Literature from the University of Milan.

Paola's poems have been included in various poetry collections, including *Desde Hong Kong: Poets in Conversation with Octavio Paz, Quixotica: Poems East of La Mancha, Mingled Voices 2, Mingled Voices 3*. She has been published in *Voice and Verse Poetry Magazine*, and has appeared in *Cha, an Asian Literary Journal* and *New Asian Writing*. Her fiction has appeared in PEN Hong Kong.

Paola is a very active poet on the local Hong Kong scene. She helps in organising special poetry nights and readings, and regularly attends Open Mic sessions. Paola "often explores the struggle and displacement of coming from the West but belonging to the East. Her poetry focuses both on the unique sights, sounds and smells of the Far East and the feelings of longing for Italy, a country undergoing challenging political and social changes."

VINCENT CASAREGOLA teaches American literature and film, creative writing, rhetorical studies, and composition. He has published poetry in a number of journals, most recently in *The Examined Life, Natural Bridge, WLA, Dappled Things, 2River, Work, Lifelines*, and *Blood and Thunder*. He was awarded the 2017 Best in Poetry Award from Blood and Thunder.

ANNE CASEY is originally from the west of Ireland and now lives in Australia. She is author of two poetry collections—*where the lost things go* (Salmon Poetry 2017) and *out of emptied cups* (Salmon Poetry 2019). Her writing and poetry rank in *The Irish Times* Most-Read.

Anne has worked for over twenty-five years as a journalist, magazine editor, media communications director and legal author. Her poetry has won or been shortlisted for awards in Ireland, the USA, the UK, Canada and Australia. She is Senior Poetry Editor of *Other Terrain Journal* and *Backstory Journal* (the two literary journals of Swinburne University, Melbourne). Anne's poems are widely published internationally—*The Irish Times*, *Entropy*, apt, Murmur House, Quiddity, Barzakh, DASH, FourXFour (Poetry Northern Ireland), Cordite, The Canberra Times, The Incubator, Verity La, Plumwood Mountain, The Honest Ulsterman, *The Stony Thursday Book*, *Into The Void*, Autonomy anthology and Burning House Press among others.

IAN JAMES CHAMBERS was born the eldest child of working-class parents in the post-war industrial north of England. His modest ancestry includes an illegitimate parent and grandparent, a Dublin prostitute, and illiterate farm labourers in Ireland's Great Famine. His Dublin-born mother managed the office of the small printing firm where his orphanage-raised father worked.

When Ian was five years old the family emigrated to Australia as "Ten Pound Poms". The long sea voyage, exotic ports of call and pioneering spirit of their new homeland had a profound impact.

Ian attempts to capture thoughts, experiences, emotions and observations through poetry, much as one uses a camera to capture a visual record—"A photograph shows what you saw but rarely conveys the full experience."—With the apparent dichotomy between his Irish Catholic roots and his scientific training, particularly in light of emotional family misfortunes (his father suffered from Parkinson's and his mother from Alzheimer's), the themes of mortality and purpose feature strongly in his work.—"I think most of us would like to feel that there's a point to our existence. For many, religion satisfies that desire, but many others must try to reconcile the incomprehensible complexity, vastness, power and beauty of the universe with the apparent insignificance and futility of human life."

An exciting career and extensive private travel have taken Ian all over the world and exposed him to numerous cultures. He has lived in England, Australia, France, The

Netherlands, Oman and the USA. Now retired, he lives in Ireland.

Ian has an honours degree in astrophysics from London University, Masters degrees in Computer Systems Management from Maryland University, and in International Relations from Cambridge. He is a fellow of the RSA and the BCS.

Following a career as a journalist and author of nonfiction books, CAROL FLAKE CHAPMAN returned to poetry, her first love, after the sudden death of her husband shattered her world. Poetry, she found, was the language of healing and of connection. Since then she has performed her poems at gatherings around the world.

CHEN FIONA YI WEN is completing her undergraduate study at The University of Hong Kong, where she is majoring in fine arts and English studies. Her interest in literature began with the experience of helping out in her secondary school library, where she was able to read inbetween volunteer hours. It was not long before her enthusiasm in writing became immense, her favourite time in school becoming the two-hour composition class. It was not until university that she started reading poetry collections, where she was once again fascinated by the lyrical beauty of words. She has only recently begun her own search for inner joy and sense of peace in poetry, and for the time being she seeks to express her feelings and love through writing.

ANNIE CHRISTAIN is an associate professor of composition and ESOL at SUNY Cobleskill and a former artist resident of the Shanghai Swatch Art Peace Hotel and the Arctic Circle Art and Science Expedition. Her poems have appeared in *Seneca Review*, *Oxford Poetry*, *The Chariton Review*, and *The Lifted Brow*, among others. She received the grand prize of the Hart Crane Memorial Poetry Contest, the Greg Grummer Poetry Award, the Oakland School of the Arts Enizagam Poetry Award, and the Neil Shepard Prize in Poetry. *Tall As You Are Tall Between*

Them, her debut poetry book, was published in the autumn of 2016 by C&R Press.

TERESA NGAN-FUNG CHU Apart from her family dogs, the poet has grown up with her mother and her two sisters, one older, one younger. Mother has been a tower of strength, always. She is the family protector and administrator. Though she has been a housewife all her life, she has had a very busy "career" looking after three human children and generations of four-legged children, all raised with tons of selfless love and round-the-clock care.

As a teenager, the poet fell in love with many brilliant poets who spoke to her inmost heart and soul. Among these were Shakespeare, T.S. Eliot, Robert Frost, Emily Dickinson and many more. During the time when the poet was in hospital after brain surgery, these poets were her only company and comfort in the many no-visitor hours. The greatest comfort came from one of Robert Frost's poems, 'The Tuft of Flowers', which filled the poet's heart and soul with gratitude for the Lord's kindness. The poet felt like the

"…tall tuft of flowers beside a brook,
A leaping tongue of bloom the scythe had spared
Beside a reedy brook the scythe had bared."

While grateful for the successful surgery, life after surgery has been tough. The brain tumour, though surgically removed, has brought with it a host of other awful illnesses that, according to the doctor, will stay with the poet for the rest of her life.

Like it or not, there are other things too the poet will have to live with for the rest of her life. C'est la vie. Yet, life goes on, and the poet will carry on, thanks to the love and support from her family, human and canine, and blessings from our Father in heaven, who has gifted her with so many beautiful verses for her life's many journeys. The poet is definitely pro-verse, and will carry on, with the Lord's given verses, to combat all the worldly curses, if and when they come.

SUZANNE COTTRELL, an Ohio buckeye by birth, lives with her husband and three rescue dogs in rural Piedmont, North Carolina. An outdoor enthusiast and retired history and special education teacher, she enjoys reading, writing, knitting, hiking, Pilates, and yoga. She loves nature's sensory stimuli and experimenting with poetry.

Her poems have appeared in numerous journals and anthologies including the *Best Emerging Poets Series*, *Avocet*, *Plum Tree Tavern*, *Poetry Quarterly*, *Haiku Journal*, *Burningword Journal*, and *The Remembered Arts Journal*. She was the recipient of the 2017 Rebecca Lard Poetry Award, Poetry Quarterly of Prolific Press.

STÉPHANE D'AMOUR is the author of four full-length collections of poems in French: L'île, 2006, shortlisted for the Prix du premier recueil de poèmes de la Fondation L.A. Finances pour la poésie (Paris), La peinture, 2008, Dans mes paysages, 2012, and À demeure, 2015.

His poems have also appeared in literary magazines and international anthologies in Québec, India, Mexico, Macedonia, Spain, and Mongolia. In 2009 he was awarded a joint grant from the Conseil des arts et des lettres du Québec and the Fondo Nacional para las Cultura y las Artes to write a book of poetry in Mexico City, about a house without walls.

Living in Hong Kong for a long while, HELEN DAVIS has developed a taste for dim sum. She always loved photography and Hong Kong offers a multitude of opportunities to take a picture. Passionate about learning how people live and what makes them tick, how people carry on in any circumstance. She finds solace in kindness, the beauty of nature and a story.

LAWDENMARC DECAMORA is a writer and researcher. His critical and literary works have been widely published in journals and magazines in the Philippines.

His work has appeared internationally in, for example, *Drunken Boat* (now *Anomaly*), *Cordite Poetry Review*, *Columbia Journal* (honorable mention, Columbia U), *Kartika Review*, SAND Journal, *The Ilanot Review* (Bar-Ilan

U, Israel), FIVE:2:ONE, aaduna, *Mithila Review*, K'in Literary Journal (Longwood U), *Subterranean Blue Poetry*, *Longleaf Review*, *Voice & Verse Poetry Magazine*, Desi Writers' Lounge's Papercuts, *The Opiate Magazine*, *Kitaab*, *Eunoia Review*, Celebration (A Gayatri Spivak-advised literary magazine), *Anak Sastra*, *Spittoon Literary Magazine*, *Peacock Journal*, *TAYO Literary Magazine*, WE ARE A WEBSITE, *The Pangolin Review*, LONTAR, AAWW's *The Transpacific Literary Project*, *Rambutan Literary*, *Shot Glass Journal*, New Reader Magazine, Mad Swirl, Chrome Baby, *New Southerner*, *In Between Hangovers*, *Panoply*, *The Conclusion Magazine*, The Ideate Review, SingPoWriMo, and *The Cadaverine*.

He holds an MFA in Creative Writing. He also teaches literature and humanities at the University of Santo Tomas- the oldest existing Catholic university in Asia. He is a serious vinyl collector of foreign and local indie music.

NEIL DOUGLAS is a doctor working in Community Paediatrics in the East End of London, UK. He is a member of the Covent Garden Stanza affiliated with the Poetry Society and has previously been published in the UK and by Proverse in the UK and Hong Kong. He has performed his poetry in London and in Hong Kong at the Proverse Spring Reception and Kubrick's.

JENNIFER EAGLETON has been a Hong Kong resident since October 1997, and has been a keen observer of Hong Kong society since her arrival in the city. In 2012 she completed a PhD on the use of metaphor in Hong Kong political discourse. Jennifer has written a number of language-related articles for Hong Kong Free Press. A previous president of the Hong Kong Women in Publishing Society, Jennifer is also a part-time tutor of stylistics/discourse analysis at the Open University of Hong Kong as well as a freelance writer, researcher, and editor on cultural topics. In her spare time she collects Hong Kong political pamphlets and artefacts.

AHMED ELBESHLAWY is a critical writer and a poet based in Hong Kong. His publications include *Savage Charm* (Proverse, 2019), *Twenty Five Meditations on Writing and Subjectivity* (London Academic Publishing, 2019), *Woman in Lars von Trier's Cinema* (Palgrave, 2016) and *America in Literature and Film* (Routledge, 2016).

C. W. EMERSON is a graduate of Fielding Graduate University and works as a clinical psychologist in Palm Springs, California. His poems appear in journals and anthologies including *Crab Orchard Review*, *december*, *Greensboro Review*, *The American Journal of Poetry*, *New Ohio Review*, *Tupelo Quarterly*. Emerson is a two-time finalist in the New Millennium Writing Awards for Poetry (2018, 2019), and has twice received an International Merit Award in the *Atlanta Review* International Poetry Competition (2017, 2018). He won Poetry International's 2018 C.P. Cavafy Poetry Prize.

RAYN EPREMIAN is a poet, filmmaker, and writer of fantasy novels, science fiction screenplays, and the occasional musical. She can most often be found in New York, the Shire, and at her website.

MATTHEW SCOTT HARRIS Born January 13th, Mcmlix
He shakes shaggy hirsute hair in utter disbelief, when nocked arrow conceived, asper their sole son, when meal ate mum and octogenarian papa begat their second offspring and only son, what now seems to be a stepped-up pace, where father time doth affix another candlebox to blow, where passage of life now measured in swiftly tailored harried styled decades denoting another birthday, when in the blink of an eye, I vividly recall crow wing like a Lil whippersnapper of a boy leisurely playing monopoly for make-believe dough...
now mere 4 fun -
a F(r)ICTIONAL BIO:
A written account (incorporates some of his self directed hyperbole). This veritable stranger now appears before your screen. Soon after reading this message, the neighbours might discern a blood curdling series of (hyena-like)

shrieking screams. No worry. That would just be the mating call of the hairy Harris mama bear. Ready! Set! Click! A scary reflection greets me whenever he summons enough steely courage to take a sneak peek into the mirror.

"Before the spider lines start to appear across the shiny surface and subsequent cracks and fissures dissolve the glassy surface, his deux hazel-coloured, myopic bespectacled eyes quickly absorb a most frightful countenance and visage. That near legendary and trademark feature of longish, wavy and brown straggly hair seems to fill the entire view. Hidden among that avant garde rhapsodic bohemian, Cro-Magnon, Neolithic, non-every-man style of un-styled locks (interspersed with silver follicles indicative of acquired worry per fighting off that garden variety prehistoric creature) can be discerned a brutish, nasty and short proto-human with a high forehead, which allows, enables and provides more skin surface to bang against the brick wall when frustrated.

"His somewhat outsize ears and longish neck (he swear exists, which contrary to popular myth never seen by living persons) support egg-shaped (fried or scrambled some might argue) head. A mostly flat and hairless chest attests to a regular regimen of light (self-concocted) chest-pounding routine. Exercise (as well as meditation) a vital part of his daily programme to deal with ordinary stresses of primitive existence. Raw coffee beans happen to be sole vice, which exotic brews provide helpful jump-start. A pair of skinny (flamingo like) legs (covered in adequate hair), now completes this general character sketch! Does this suffice?

"After attempting to envision some vague essential apparition or near facsimile of what barely passes muster as a Caucasian male, I wonder if you happen to be less or more favorably disposed toward some healthy interaction of body, mind and spirit.

"Now if you would politely excuse me, I MUST scavenge for some berries, exotic tree bark or that stray small and wild game some gremlins will not be a cannibal for eat me far away by the bay any day, but best wait for one overcast and fifty shades of gray ideal month would be May."'

KATE HAWKINS, originally from Australia, has spent over half her life living in Hong Kong. She is an actor, voice-over artist, and poet, as well as an award-winning television presenter and scriptwriter. She co-edited and was published in two Hong Kong Writers' Circle anthologies, *Another Hong Kong* and *Hong Kong Gothic*, and has been published in two Proverse poetry anthologies, *Mingled Voices 2* and *Mingled Voices 3*. Kate has a degree in Creative Writing from Queensland University of Technology and has been writing for as long as she can remember.

DAH HELMER's seventh poetry collection is Something Else's Thoughts (Transcendent Zero Press) and his poems have been published by editors from the US, UK, Ireland, Canada, Nigeria, Spain, Singapore, Poland, Philippines, Australia, Africa, India, and Italy. He is the lead editor for the poetry critique group, The Lounge. Dah's eighth book is *Full Life In The Day Of A Poet* (Cyberwit Press, 2019).

AIDEN HEUNG is a native Chinese poet born and raised on the edge of the Tibetan Plateau; He holds an MA in literature at Tongji University in Shanghai where he currently works and lives. His poems have been published in many online and offline magazines, most notably in *Literary Shanghai*, *The Shanghai Literary Review*, *Cha: An Asian Literary Journal*, *New English Review*, *Anak Sastra*, *Mascara Literary Review*, among many others. He is an avid reader who writes both in English and Chinese. He can be found at Aiden-Heung.com or www.twitter.com/aidenheung

CARRIE HOOPER was born and raised in Elmira, New York, where she currently lives. She received a Bachelor's degree in music performance from Mansfield University (Mansfield, Pennsylvania) and Master's degrees in German and vocal performance from the University of Buffalo (Buffalo, New York). She studied for one year at the Royal University College of Music in Stockholm, Sweden, as a Fulbright Scholar.

She taught German at Elmira College from 2002 until 2019 and also taught Italian there for a number of years. She teaches voice and piano at Studios on the Square in Horseheads, New York. She also serves as pianist and organist at St. Matthew's Episcopal Church in Horseheads. She is a member of the Common Time Choral Group. Carrie gives vocal concerts in different venues in the area.

In addition to teaching and other musical activities, Carrie enjoys learning foreign languages. She is proficient in German, Italian, Spanish, Swedish, Albanian, and Romanian. In 2018 she published a collection of poetry in Albanian with English translations entitled Word Paintings

R.J. KEELER was born in St. Paul, Minnesota, but lived in the jungles of Colombia, South America, up to the age of twelve. His formal studies include: Duke University; BS Mathematics North Carolina State University; MS Computer Science University of North Carolina at Chapel Hill; MBA University of California at Los Angeles; Certificate in Poetry University of Washington. Honorman, U.S. Naval Submarine School. "SS" (Submarine Service) qualified. Vietnam Service Medal. Honorable Discharge. Member Institute of Electrical and Electronics Engineers, American Association for the Advancement of Science, Academy of American Poets. The Boeing Company engineer..

ZACHARY TAYLOR KNOX has had poems published in *Ealain*, *Scum Gentry Poetryhole*, *What Rough Beast*, and the *Mingled Voices 3* anthology. He lives in Fort Madison, Iowa with his family.

LYNDA LAMBERT lives in Wurtemburg (Perry Township), Western PA. She is a retired Professor of Fine Arts & Humanities at Geneva College, Beaver Falls, PA. She lectured in art history and gave conference presentations in art and literature. She taught English Literature; studio art; and a month-long summer course in Europe each year.

SUSAN LAVENDER is a Hong Kong-based published poet, actress, radio broadcaster, lawyer and Italian translator. She performs in theatre and commercial filming, story-telling and literary events, such as the Hong Kong Literary Festival, Hong Kong Spoken Word Festival and Liars' League HK.

She often writes her own material, including performance poetry combining her acting with creative writing. She is a regular contributor to Proverse Hong Kong, Cha Asian Literary Journal, Hong Kong Peel St. Poetry and Poetry Outloud.   Anglo-Italian by birth, Susan has lived in Hong Kong and China for 27 years. She is bilingual in English and Italian, fluent in French and has also studied Mandarin and Cantonese.

IRIS LITT's newest book of poems is *Snowbird* from Finishing Line Press. Previous books are *What I Wanted to Say* from Shivastan Press, and *Word Love* from Cosmic Trend Publications. A recent short story publication is 'Pissed Off' in the *Saturday Evening Post* Fiction Contest Anthology. She has had short stories, poems and articles in *Saturday Evening Post, Travelers' Tales, Confrontation, The Widow's Handbook, The London Magazine, the new renaissance, Earth's Daughters, Rambunctious Review* and many others. Awards include the *Atlantic Monthly* Award for College Writing, first prize in The Virtual Press short story contest, French Bread poetry award from *Pacific Coast Journal*.

She has taught creative writing as an adjunct at SUNY/Ulster, Bard College, Arts Society of Kingston, Writers in the Mountains, New York Public Library and many other venues in New York City and the Hudson Valley.

She lives in Woodstock, NY and winters on Anna Maria Island in Florida, which was the inspiration for *Snowbird*.

WAYNE PAUL MATTINGLY is a multi-award-winning playwright whose work has been staged in NYC; Westchester & Putnam Counties, N.Y; Los Angeles, San Francisco; Bangor, Maine; Denton & Houston, Texas; Chamblee, GA; Valdez, Alaska; Kauai, Hawaii; and London, England.

His work has been recognised as follows: Winner of the 2007 Tennessee Chapbook Prize; 2011 Arts & Letters Prize in Drama, Finalist, Milledgeville, GA; 2012 Denton Community Theatre, Method and Madness Competition & Festival, 3rd Prize, Denton, TX; 2012 The Last Frontier Theatre Conference,/Susan Nims Distinguished Play Playwright Award Finalist, Valdez, Alaska; 2012 Phoenix Theatre, Hormel New Play Festival Finalist; 2013 The Ashland New Plays Festival Semi-finalist, Ashland, OR; 2014 Ronald Duncan Literary Prize Finalist, United Kingdom; and 25th Annual International Playwriting Festival, Warehouse Theatre Co., London, U.K. and an IATC 2016 Cimientos Play Development Program Finalist, NYC.

He is proud to have been awarded a 2014 Helene Wurlitzer Foundation Fellowship Artists Residency Grant, Taos, NM; & to be a Grant Recipient of the 2014 & 2015 Disquiet International Literary Programs (Short Plays), in Lisbon, Portugal; and both a 2015/16 Can Serrat, and 2017/18 Can Serrat International Artists Residency Grant Recipient, in Barcelona, Spain.

He was a founding member & Dramaturg of The Misfits Ensemble in L.A., Founding Artistic Director of Tiger's Heart Players in N.Y, a Dramatist Guild, & Actors' Equity Association member. Last seen on stage in the 2013 Midtown International Theatre Festival in NYC, he was nominated for a Best Lead Actor Award. He has directed well over two dozen works both in CA & NY. His newest full length drama, Anthem, was read at both The Village Playwrights in NYC & Axial Theatre in Ossining, NY.

His published work can be found in 2017 The Best 10-Minute Plays, Smith & Kraus; 2015 Applause Theatre & Cinema Books; 2014 Best Women's Monologues Smith & Kraus; 2007 Poetry & Plays 14; Best Women's Monologues 1999 & Best Stage Scenes, 1999, Smith & Kraus. Some work is available through the National New Play Network.

BRITTANY MISHRA helps make airplane engines for a living and writes poetry and fiction as her passion. Originally from the Pacific Northwest, she now lives in New Britain, Connecticut with her husband. Brittany's poetry can be found in Shabda Press' *Nuclear Impact Anthology* and the online journals *Voice Catcher*, *Sky Island*, *The Write Launch*, and *Typishly*.

RONY NAIR is a poet, photographer and a part-time columnist. His professional photography has been exhibited and been featured in several literary journals. His poetry, photography and writings have previously been featured by the *Chiron Review*, *Modern Literature*, *The Indian Express*, *Modern Literature*, YGDRASIL journal, *Mindless Muse*, *Yellow Chair Review*, *Two Words For*, *Alephi*, *New Asian Writing* (NAW), *Semaphore*, *The Economic Times*, 1947, *The Foliate Oak Magazine*, *Open Road*, *Tipton Review*, *Antarctica Journal*, *North East Review*, *Indian Literature*, and *Coldnoon*, among many others. Rony has exhibited his art widely and continues to work on his non-fiction and poetry projects.

KEITH NUNES (New Zealand) was nominated for Best Small Fictions 2019, the Pushcart Prize and won the 2017 Flash Frontier Short Fiction Award. He's had poetry, haiku, short fiction, Asemic Writing and Foto-Poetry published around the globe. His poetry book *catching a ride on a paradox* is out there.

HELEN OLIVER is an ESL teacher, materials writer and editor. Working part-time now allows more time for tai qi, music, books and poetry, family and friends. She loves the sea, kayaking and wandering the beaches of New Zealand. Writing is becoming a passion.

PATIENCE O'NEILL is fascinated by the creative process, with its alchemy of intuition and writer's craft revealing insights into ourselves and our relationships with each other. She believes we are story-telling beings. We need stories to make sense of our existence.

RENA ONG is a retired teacher of children with Dyslexia. She was born and grew up in England and has lived in Singapore for 35 years with her Singaporean husband. Their grown-up son lives in Melbourne, Australia. This poem reflects that, though we may be living far apart, love binds, love heals and love is forever. Her writings are inspired from her emotional and spiritual experiences or observations of others having such experiences. She hopes to give a voice to feelings that often cannot be expressed.

JUN (JANICE) PAN is an interpreter, translator, researcher and interpreter and translator trainer. With a passion for reading and writing, she founded a Chinese poetry club and published a couple of Chinese poems (shi and ci) at the age of twelve at her birthplace in Xiangtan, Hunan. She then studied English language and literature in Jiangsu and interpreting in Shanghai. She came to Hong Kong in 2008 for her PhD on interpreting studies and has been teaching interpreting and translation at local tertiary institutions since then.

Jun has worked as an interpreter (and translator) for many years, although her childhood dream was to become a writer, director or painter. She found her childhood immersion in Chinese classic literature and culture important and invaluable in her life and career.

Apart from introducing Chinese culture to many of her clients when she worked as an interpreter, Jun also participated in the translation of several classic works from English to Chinese, including John Ruskin's five-volumed *Modern Painters,* Lyman Frank Baum's *The Wonderful Wizard of Oz* and *The Marvelous Land of Oz,* etc.

Jun is now Associate Professor in the Translation Programme and Director of the M.A. Programme in Translation and Bilingual Communication at Hong Kong Baptist University. She has also been playing Guqin (Chinese seven-stringed zither) during the past seven years, which, according to her, helps her to find an inner peace in her constant struggle and search for a balance between an oriental and occidental cultural identity.

ANDY PEYRIE is an autodidact who started writing to ameliorate the boredom of some of his paying (yet nevertheless unmonitored) jobs. He has been published on WordRiot and The Voices Project.

MARTIN JON PORTER grew up in Ballarat and studied teaching in Adelaide, but now lives in Melbourne with his family. His poems have been published in Australia, Canada, USA, UK and online. His first full-length collection, *No Home Like a Raft*, has recently been published by Atmosphere Press.

SIMONA RACKOVÁ (b. 1976) is a poet, editor, literary critic and journalist. She graduated with an MA in Czech Language and Literature at the Philosophical Faculty of the Charles University in Prague.

Since 2013, she has been the head editor of the Review Department at the prestigious art and literary magazine *Tvar*. She also edited an annual publication *Sto nejlepších českých básní* 2012 (One Hundred Best Czech Poems; Host Publishers) and the two-volume Antologie české poezie in 2007 and 2009 respectively (An Anthology of Czech Poetry; dybbuk Publishers).

Her debut poetry collection *Přítelkyně* (Girlfriends; in the Literární salon Publisher, Prague) came out in 2007. Her collection of twelve poems about Venice, *Město, které není* (A City that Doesn't Exist), accompanied by linocuts of Pavel Piekar, was printed privately as a small-run publication in 2009. It was followed by the 2015 collection *Tance* (Dances, Dauphin Publ., Prague). She is the 2016 winner of the international Dresden Lyrical Prize.

The presented poems come from the collection *Tance*. Simona's latest collection *Zatímco hlídací psi spí* was published in September 2017 (While the Guard Dogs Are Asleep; Dauphin Publ., Prague).

She lives with her husband and two children in Prague.

JOANNA RADWAŃSKA-WILLIAMS was born in Warsaw, Poland, and spent a part of her childhood in London, England. She received her B.A. with a double major in English and Linguistics (awarded with Highest Honors) and her Ph.D. in Linguistics from the University of North Carolina at Chapel Hill. Her dissertation was published as *A Paradigm Lost: The Linguistic Theory of Mikołaj Kruszewski* (Amsterdam: John Benjamins, 1993). She taught Slavic Linguistics (Polish and Russian) at the

State University of New York at Stony Brook (1989-1994) and the University of Illinois at Chicago (1994-1995), and English Linguistics at Nanjing University (1996-1999) and the Chinese University of Hong Kong (1999-2003). In 2003, she joined Macao Polytechnic Institute, where she is now a full professor at the MPI-Bell Centre of English.

Joanna's poetry has been anthologized in several collections, including *Lingua Franca: An Anthology of Poetry by Linguists* (edited by Donna Jo Napoli and Emily Norwood Rando; Lake Bluff, Illinois: Jupiter Press, 1989), *Montage of Life* (Owings Mills, Maryland: The National Library of Poetry, 1998), *I Roll the Dice: Contemporary Macao Poetry* (edited by Christopher Kit Kelen and Agnes Vong; Macao: Association of Stories in Macao, 2008), *Lotus Field 2018: Reflections* (edited by Zi-yu Lin, Joanna Radwańska-Williams and Yunfeng Zhang; Macao: Macao Polytechnic Institute, 2018), *Mingled Voices 2: International Proverse Poetry Prize Anthology 2017* and *Mingled Voices 3: International Proverse Poetry Prize Anthology 2018* (edited by Gillian Bickley and Verner Bickley; Hong Kong: Proverse Hong Kong, 2018, 2019).

C.N. RAJALAKSHMI (RAJI) is a poet and Language Teacher living in Hong Kong with her family. Her facebook page, "Raji's Poetic World", attracts an international audience. Raji's poetry explores culture and nature with deep underlying philosophies, inspired by human nature, religion and natural sceneries. For her, "Poetry is an artistic expression of the self". Her poems have appeared in various international anthologies and online platforms and she has read her work on RTHK. While not at work, she loves travelling and reading.

HARSH RAMCHANDANI is a graduate of Media Arts and a hobby writer based in Hong Kong. He primarily enjoys writing poetry and flash fiction. You can find some of his writing, photography and art on his website.

PATRICK T. REARDON is the author of eight books, including the poetry collection *Requiem for David* and *Faith Stripped to Its Essence*, a literary-religious analysis of

Shusaku Endo's novel *Silence*. His poetry has appeared in *Silver Birch Press*, *Cold Noon*, *Eclectica*, *Esthetic Apostle*, *Ground Fresh Thursday*, *Literary Orphans*, *Rhino*, *Spank the Carp*, *Main Street Rag*, *Down in the Dirt*, *Time for Singing*, *Tipton Poetry Journal*, *Under a Warm Green Linden* and *The Write City*. Reardon, who worked as a *Chicago Tribune* reporter for 32 years, has published essays and book reviews widely in such publications as the *Tribune*, *Chicago Sun-Times*, *Crain's Chicago Business*, *National Catholic Reporter* and *U.S. Catholic*. His novella *Babe* was short-listed by Stewart O'Nan for the annual Faulkner-Wisdom Contest.

M. ANN REED is a poet, Chinese calligrapher-brush painter and professor of English Literature and Theory of Knowledge. She has taught in Malaysia, Ukraine, Bosnia-Herzegovina and China where traditional cultures regard literature a medical art. Her postdoctoral research studies the mending arts of Early Modern English and Contemporary Poetry. Her Chinese calligraphy and brush paintings have been exhibited in Portland, Oregon and at the Shenzhen Fine Arts Museum in China. Her poems have been published in various literary journals.

VINNI RELWANI resides in Singapore, and enjoys writing poetry and short stories, a few of which have found their way into the publishing realm.

ANGELO RIZZI was born in 1956, in Sant'Angelo Lodigiano, Italy. His mother tongue is Italian, but he is a polyglot poet, writing in Arabic, Italian and French. He has published fourteen collections of poems, the most recent being, *Lemhat al-hidâ'ati* (bilingual) (The profile of the kite), ed. BoD, 2018.

He has received many literary awards, such as the prestigious Nosside World Prize in 2004. In 2016, the Academia Internacional de Ciéncias, Létras and Art ALPAS XXI in Cruz Alta (Porto Alegre), R/S Brazil, nominated him International Correspondent Academic. He received the first Award for poetry in foreign language at « Città di Voghera », (Italy) 2019. As well as four Critics' Awards and many

Honorable Mentions and Special Mentions, he has been a Finalist in Italy, Spain, Switzerland, Venezuela, Argentina, U.S.A.

He has participated in international poetry meetings and recitals in Rome (Italy), Havana (Cuba), Paris, Breil-sur-Roya, Mouans-Sartoux (France), Monaco, Curtea de Argeş (Romanía) and Djerba (Tunisia). In 2006, he attended the UNESCO Congress, "Dialogue among the Nations".

Rizzi is a member of REMES (Red Mundial de Escritores en Español); World Poets Society; Poetas del Mundo and SELAE (Sociedad de Escritores Latino-Americanos y Europeos).

His poems have appeared in anthologies and magazines in Italy, the United States, Switzerland, Cuba, Argentina, Spain, Kuwait, Brazil, Romania, Hong Kong, and India. He has collaborated with the multi-language magazine, *A Oriente* (Milan, 2000, 2001).

He has published fifteen collections of poems.

APARNA UPADHYAYA SANYAL has an MA from Kings College, London. Her debut book, *Circus Folk & Village Freaks* (Sept 2018) has since been ranked Number One on both the "Poetry Bestseller" List and the "Hot New Releases" List, on Amazon India. She is the recipient of the 14th Beullah Rose Poetry Prize by Smartish Pace. She was shortlisted for the 2018 Third Coast Fiction Prize. She has poetry in *The Penn Review*, *Smartish Pace*, *Dunes Review*, SOFTBLOW, *Typehouse Literary Review*, *Vayavya*, and many more. A popular Spoken Word poet, she performs at events across venues in India. She lives with her 5-year-old son, husband and two puppies in Pune, India.

HALIL SUAT SARAÇ is 23 years old and has recently graduated from Boğaziçi University Psychology Department. He is endeavoring to translate *Hamlet* into Turkish, writes poems in both Turkish and English, and is working on a play. His passion lies in discovering the long-short journey of the human species. In this journey, he is especially interested in language capacity and psychosis.

ALLEGRA JOSTAD SILBERSTEIN grew up on a farm in Wisconsin but has lived in California since 1963. Her love of poetry began as a child when her mother would recite poems as she worked. Now that she is retired there is more time for singing and dancing as well as poetry. She has published three chapbooks of poetry. In the spring of 2015, Cold River Press published her first book and she is widely published in journals such as *Blue Unicorn*, *California Quarterly*, *Iodine Poetry* and *Poetry Now*. In March of 2010 she was honored to become the first Poet Laureate for the city of Davis, CA.

HAYLEY ANN SOLOMON is a professional author and poet. She spent many years of her life as an academic librarian and is the mother of three delightful sons. They are now all grown up and much cleverer than her! Hayley is delighted to twice be a recipient of the Proverse Supplementary Prize and spends much of each day singing. She is currently studying for her ATCL in music but is never far from the development of a new novel or poem.

ABBIE JOHNSON TAYLOR is the author of two novels, two poetry collections, and a memoir. Besides the Proverse Poetry anthologies, her work has appeared in *Magnets and Ladders*, *The Avocet*, and other publications. She has a visual impairment and lives in Sheridan, Wyoming, where for six years, she cared for her late husband, who was totally blind and partially paralyzed by two strokes.

LUISA TERNAU was born and raised in Trieste, in the Italian North-East. After graduating from the University of Trieste, she moved to London where she gained a Master in English Literature at King's College, University of London. She then moved to live and work successively in Japan, US, and Hong Kong where she is currently based.

She has always loved poetry and likes to read poems from all nations and traditions. The inspiration of her poetry comes from her love and observation of life. Her poems appear in anthologies published in Hong Kong. In 2016 she was awarded a third prize in the International Proverse Poetry Prize competition.

EDWARD TIESSE recently returned to Washington State after living for several years in the Chicago area. From his home, on clear days, he can see Mount Baker and the Canadian Cascades. Living so close to Canada makes it easy to slip across the border when it becomes necessary. He has many interests. He loves to cook and recently began baking bread which he soon learned is much like writing poetry. That is, the combinations of flour, water and yeast have many variables and so baking is much like trying to find the right word and its correct place in a line. Edward's poetry has been published in *The Front Porch Review*, *The Sea Letter* and the Proverse Anthologies.

DEEPA VANJANI has been an academic for more than two decades and now heads the English department in a college in Indore, central India. Having freelanced with the *Hindustan Times* and the *Times of India* for some years, she now writes for *Confluence: South Asian Perspectives*, published from London. In 2016, Proverse Hong Kong published her poetry collection, *Shifting Sands*. Deepa is an animal lover and has been working for their welfare for the past several years.

PETER COE VERBICA grew up on a commercial cattle ranch in Northern California. He obtained a BA and JD from Santa Clara University and an MS from the Massachusetts Institute of Technology. He is married and has four daughters.

ANSON HONGHUA WANG is an Assistant Professor in Translation. Her research interests are interpreter and translator training, gender and translation and second language acquisition. She is a practicing translator and interpreter. Besides research, she has a wide range of interests including reading, watching movies and hiking. She has been serving as Executive Committee Member of the Hong Kong Association of University Women since 2013. She is also a member of International Association for Translation and Intercultural Studies.

BRUCE ARLEN WASSERMAN assembled his first poetry manuscript at the age of seventeen and later farmed and worked as a blacksmith in his twenties and as an editor through graduate school. He received his MFA from Vermont College of Fine Arts.

His poems have been published in *Mingled Voices 2* and *Mingled Voices 3* (the 2017 and 2018 *Proverse Poetry Prize Anthologies*), *The Fredericksburg Literary and Art Review*, *The River Heron Review*, *Kindred Literary Magazine* and *Broad River Review*.

He is a book critic for the *New York Journal of Books* and the *Washington Independent Review of Books* and a Graduate Assistant at the MFA in Writing programme of Vermont College of Fine Arts. At other times, he creates visual art as a potter at the Bruce Arlen Wasserman Studio, or performs as a musician in a band. On occasion, he trains horses.

GEORGE WATT is a retired professor who has published a number of books in literary criticism and language education. He has only recently discovered the joys and trials of writing poetry, which in equal measure is both surprising and uplifting.

MOCCO WOLLERT was born in Cologne, Germany. In 1958, she migrated to Australia with her husband, first settling in Darwin NT, but moving to Queensland in 1972.

She has been widely published in Literary Anthologies, Newspapers (*Sydney Morning Herald*) Magazines (*The Bulletin*) and Literary Journals (*Redoubt*). In 1980 she founded the Queensland Branch of The Society of Women Writers, and remains an active member. She has won many prizes and awards for her poetry, short stories and articles, most recently (2017) 1st prize in the Eaglehawk Dahlia national poetry competition.

Mocco has ten published poetry books to her credit: Published by the SWWQ: *Jacaranda Time.* Published by Boolarong Press: *She is a Cat, With open Arms, Reflections on Crystal Water, Fly Spirit Bird Fly,*

Published by Interactive Publications: *Love Falls in Love
with Love, Of Loving and Sensualities, Australia Images and
Inspiration.*
Self-published: *The Beating of Wings*
Her memoir, *Bloody Bastard Beautiful*, was published by
the Historical Society of N.T. in July 2017 and republished
by Boolarong Press in Brisbane in November 2017.
  Mocco writes in English and German.

WONG SUK MAN (Maggie) was born in Hong Kong and
is a graduate of the Chinese University of Hong Kong. She
worked in different fields before becoming a teacher.
Teaching fulfils her desire to help young people equip
themselves. It also gives her the drive continuously to learn
and make progress. She started writing English poems eight
years ago and has written more than seven hundred poems
since then. Besides being an avid reader and writer, she's
also a keen runner. She was 1st runner-up in the 10KM
Women's Master 2 in the Standard Chartered Hong Kong
Marathon in 2016 and 2017, and 2nd runner-up in 2019.
Hong Kong is her hometown and her love for the city will
never die.

MARJORY WOODFIELD is a New Zealand teacher and
writer who has recently returned from living in the Middle
East. She has been published by the BBC, Raven
Chronicles, Cargo Literary, Flash Frontier, Meniscus and
others. She won the 2019 Dunedin UNESCO City of
Literature Robert Burns Poetry Competition and received a
commendation in the 2019 Hippocrates Open Awards for
Poetry and Medicine. She has been anthologized by
Frogmore Press in *Pale Fire—New Writing on the Moon.*

THE EDITORS

GILLIAN BICKLEY, born and educated in the United Kingdom, has lived mostly in Hong Kong since 1970. She has been a member of the Society of Authors in the United Kingdom since her school days.

Her poetry collections include *For the Record and other Poems of Hong Kong*, *Moving House and other Poems from Hong Kong*, *Sightings*, *China Suite*, *Perceptions* and the bilingual English-Romanian *Poems/Poeme*. Two collections—*Moving House* and *For the Record*—have also been published in Chinese; individual poems have been published in Arabic, Catalan, Chinese, Czech, French, German, Romanian, Turkish and other languages. *Over the Years* (2017) is a selection from her previously published work, selected by Verner Bickley. In 2014, she was awarded the "Grand Prix Orient-Occident Des Arts" at the 18th International Festival, "Curtea de Argeş Poetry Nights", held in Romania. Gillian Bickley is one of the Hong Kong poets discussed in Agnes S. L. Lam's study, *Becoming poets: The Asian English Experience*.

Gillian has written or edited several non-fiction books in different fields: *The Golden Needle: The Biography of Frederick Stewart, 1836-1889 (founder of Hong Kong Government Education)*, Hong Kong Baptist University and David C. Lam Institute for East-West Studies, 1997; *Hong Kong Invaded! A '97 Nightmare*, University of Hong Kong Press, Hong Kong, 2001; *The Development of Education in Hong Kong, 1841-1897: as revealed through the Early Education Reports of the Hong Kong Government, 1848-1896*, Proverse Hong Kong, Hong Kong, 2002; *The Stewarts of Bourtreebush*, Centre for Scottish Studies, University of Aberdeen, Scotland, 2003; *A Magistrate's Court in 19th Century Hong Kong: Court in Time*, Proverse Hong Kong, first edition, 2005; second edition, 2009; *The Complete Court Cases of Magistrate Frederick Stewart*, Proverse Hong Kong, 2008; *In Time of War* (in collaboration with Richard Collingwood-Selby), an edition based on the writings of Henry C.S. Collingwood-Selby (1898-1992), Lieutenant Commander in the Royal Navy, Proverse Hong Kong, 2013, *Through American Eyes: The Journals of*

George Washington (Farley) Heard (1837-1875), Proverse Hong Kong, 2017; *Journeys with a Mission: Travel Journals of The Right Revd George Smith (1815-1871), first Bishop of Victoria, Hong Kong (1849-1865)*, Proverse Hong Kong, 2018.

Five of these fourteen English-language books received publication support from Hong Kong Arts Development Council (HKADC) and four from the Lord Wilson Heritage Trust. The extensive research necessary for seven of the non-fiction works listed was made possible by research grants awarded by the Hong Kong Baptist University and one was supported by a private sponsor.

She has been a member of the Society of Authors, UK, since she was a schoolgirl.

Dr Bickley was Senior Lecturer / Associate Professor in the Department of English at the Hong Kong Baptist University for twenty-two years. She has been a full-time faculty member at the University of Lagos, Nigeria; the University of Auckland, New Zealand; and at the University of Hong Kong.

For several years, Gillian was an adjudicator at the world-famous Hong Kong Schools Music & Speech Association's annual Speech Festival and has also been a judge for the Budding Poets' Society Hong Kong.

More recently, as co-ordinator of literary activities for the English-Speaking Union Hong Kong, a non-profit registered educational charity, she has led reading appreciation sessions which are open to the community and assists to deliver reading courses at local schools. She has worked with the Gifted Education Section of the Education Bureau to encourage creative writing among students. On a freelance basis, she has taught creative reading / writing courses at the Hong Kong Academy for Gifted Education (HKAGE) and at the University of Hong Kong School for Professional and Continuing Education (HKU SPACE) and been a guest lecturer on poetry at Lingnan University Community College. Her creative reading / writing course at HKU SPACE continues to be offered. In 2016, she managed twenty and hosted seventeen meet-the-author events at a Hong Kong bookshop. On occasion, she accepts invitations to speak at school Reading Festivals and similar.

Following her career in academia, Gillian has become an experienced publisher, project-manager, text editor, and production manager, including of poetry, non-fiction, fiction and academic writing. She has been President of the Hong Kong Association of University Women and has recently stepped aside from her role as a Vice-President of the Royal Asiatic Society (Hong Kong).

THE EDITORS

VERNER BICKLEY was born in the North-West of England, and educated there, in Wales and London, and has lived in Asian and Pacific countries for over fifty years.

He has been scholar, teacher, manager, broadcaster, stage and film actor and cultural diplomat in a life often enlivened by music and song, dance and entertainment.

Verner's many scholarly articles and book publications are mainly on educational and cross-cultural topics. He has however also published two volumes of memoirs: *Footfalls Echo in the Memory* and *Steps To Paradise And Beyond*. His five-book graded poetry anthology, *Poems to Enjoy*, has been popular since the 1960s. These now benefit from accompanying recordings of all poems in the texts (read mostly by himself, but some by his wife, Gillian), as well as from teaching and performance notes. He is a member of the United Kingdom Society of Authors.

With his wife, Gillian, Verner Bickley is joint-publisher of Proverse Hong Kong and co-founder of the Proverse Prize and the Proverse Poetry Prize.

Verner was a naval officer in pre-independent Sri Lanka and India. He served in the Colonial Education Service in Singapore and, later, as a British Council officer in post-independence Burma, Indonesia and Japan. In Hawaii from 1971 to 1981, he served as the Director of the Culture Learning Institute at the East-West Center, established by the US Congress in Hawaii in 1960 and functioning as a US-based institution for public diplomacy with international governance, staffing, students and Fellows.

From 1972 to 1980, Verner led a small team of anthropologists, cross-cultural psychologists and linguists, focusing on the different ways in which individuals and whole societies cope in bicultural and multicultural contexts and how they address problems presented by different cultural norms. Among many interesting projects, his Institute provided for the pioneering voyage of the canoe, *Hõküle'a*, from Hawaii to Tahiti, disproving the theories of Thor Heyerdahl.

Verner was instrumental in bringing to conferences in Honolulu writers who included Guy Amirthanayagam, Leon Edel, Vincent Eri, Nissim Ezekial, Reuel Denney, Janet Frame, Allen Ginsberg, Syd Harrex, Thomas Keneally, Maxine Hong-Kingston, Arun Kolatkhar, Ananda Murthy, Kenzaburo Oe, Kushwant Singh, Kamala Markandaya, R.K. Narayan, A.K. Ramanajuan, E.R. Sarachchandra, Wole Soyinka and Albert Wendt.

After leaving Hawaii, and while in Saudia Arabia for a two-year assignment with the national airline, Saudia, Verner was responsible for a multi-national staff of 100 persons, mainly, but not exclusively, in Jeddah and Riyadh.

In 1983, Verner was appointed founding director of the Institute of Language in Education in Hong Kong and held that post until 1992.

Refusing to retire, Verner continues to live in Hong Kong where he writes and publishes on a variety of topics. He was founding Chairman of the English-Speaking Union (Hong Kong) and continued as Chairman of the Executive Committee for sixteen years. He recently passed this responsibility over to a new chairman, but in his capacity as Chairman Emeritus continues with his own portfolio of tasks. As Chairman, he traveled for many years to the Mainland of China to join other judges of the national Public-Speaking Competition organised by national media. He was an adjudicator for the Hong Kong Schools Music and Speech Association's annual Speech Festival for many years and for a while was Representative in Hong Kong for Trinity College London.

Verner Bickley's experiences have created in him an interest in cross-cultural experiences and attitudes and in a desire to communicate what he has learnt. Through his memoirs as well as his personal contacts, he hopes not only to interest others, but to encourage them to build on their own desire to learn about and empathise with other cultures.

PROVERSE HONG KONG

Together, Gillian and Verner Bickley are the publishers of Proverse Hong Kong, a Hong Kong-based press which publishes both local and international authors, including non-native speakers of English. They are also co-founders of two annual international literary prizes for work submitted in English: in 2008, they founded the Proverse Prize for unpublished book-length fiction, non-fiction or poetry, and, in 2016, they established the Proverse Poetry Prize (for single poems which may have been previously published in a language other than English). In the case of both prizes, entries are received from around the world.

Beginning in 2007 up to December 2019, Proverse has managed, edited and published about 126 English-language books by Hong Kong and international writers, five Chinese-language books and one English / Chinese bilingual book. Of the English-language books, about nineteen have been awarded publication support by Hong Kong Arts Development Council (HKADC), four by Lord Wilson Heritage Trust and one by the Ride Fund for publication in the Royal Asiatic Society Hong Kong Studies series. One received a publication grant from the Ministry of Culture of the Czech Republic and one received a publication grant from the Ministry of Culture and Tourism of the Republic of Turkey.

Twice a year, Proverse organises literary events in Hong Kong, open to the public. New books are launched, writers are introduced and launching authors give brief talks. Announcements are made relating to the current year's Proverse Prize for unpublished fiction, non-fiction or poetry, and the Proverse Poetry Prize (for single short poems); their prizes are presented to those winning authors who are present. Videos of a couple of these events are available on Youtube and photos of most of them are available on the Proverse website, proversepublishing.com.

Gillian and Verner work hard to bring authors before the reading public and to encourage reading. On three occasions, they have administered Reading Development Grants awarded by the Hong Kong Arts Development Council. In 2016, as implementation of one of these, they arranged twenty meet-the-author sessions, held at a Hong Kong bookshop. To reach an international audience, edited videos of these talks are available on Youtube.

Of the titles published by Proverse, several have attracted a Preface or advance appreciation from figures of international reputation, most notably perhaps, from Václav Havel (for the English translation of Olga Walló's *Tightrope: A Bohemian Tale*).

Two titles (Peter Gregoire's, *Article 109* and *The Devil You Know*) were best sellers at Dymocks Hong Kong.

The publication by Proverse of the late Sophronia Liu's book, *A Shimmering Sea*, was a major argument in the award to Sophronia of a posthumous PhD at the University of Minnesota.

Other writers published by Proverse have also benefited in their literary careers, a couple of them taking a leadership role in local literary groups.

Gillian's and Verner's own books and all those by other authors published by Proverse, are available internationally as well as locally, including through the Chinese University of Hong Kong Press. There are copies in the British Library and other legal deposit libraries in the United Kingdom, and in the Hong Kong Public Library system, as well as in many university and public libraries world-wide.

POETS' NOTES AND COMMENTARIES

[1] Joy Al-Sofi writes this about her poem, 'Alive'. "There are times when urban dwellers can forget they are living in a biologic and natural world, that they are connected to the rest of life. But once in a while something can take you away from what you are used to and you are brought face to face with a very different aspect of life, one that is exciting, strange and terrifying. These are times when you are presented with choices. You can either reject the experience and keep it at a distance, in the way you would observe a remote galaxy through a telescope or a far away star. Or you can see your commonality, yourself in the other, sometimes almost literally.

"When making videos of my wildlife sightings, I go through my images more carefully and repeatedly than in years past. In looking at images from my trip this year to the Chobe river in Botswana, I was struck by the reflectivity of the eyes of Nile crocodiles who were very, very close to us. Reflecting on those eyes led to this poem."

[2] Of her poem, 'Holiday!', Joy Al-Sofi writes: "I like to travel and sometimes it's just fun, but in thinking about the places I have visited in recent years, it became clear that one of those choices, Africa, changed me and altered my life's direction and focus. I pondered whether this happens to others, and how often. What state of mind or location might have that effect on others. How often a holiday (the word coming from 'holy day'), is exactly what you expected. But, there are times when we simply don't know the consequences of what we may start out thinking is of little consequence."

[3] Sui Ping Au Yeung explains that her poem, 'Sailing' " is ... for Marco Leung Ling-Kit, who is the first martyr of the Anti-Extradition Bill protest in Hong Kong. His yellow raincoat scattered in the sky. I hope that thousands of anonymous waves will continue to fight for justice."

[4] Reema Baniabbasi writes this about her poem, 'Plastic Violence': "I grew up having difficulty connecting as a sensitive introvert in a fast changing city of superlatives like Dubai. A decade away being trained as a counseling psychologist in Boston introduced me to diverse ways of being which was the environment I needed to nourish my self esteem. I found that not only was I much better in touch with my emotions, but I was also able to connect much more effortlessly. 'Plastic Violence' was written after my recent return to Dubai when I finally developed the language to describe the violence I saw people perpetuating against themselves which in turn translates to larger violences that we are all complicit in."

[5] Thea Biesheuvel wrote this about her poem, 'Sempiternity': "The poem highlights and to a certain extent celebrates the fresh look we get when we move to new locations, whether these moves are voluntary or forced. Many 'newcomers' to a country feel they are strangers in a strange land. They can see the double-edged landscape, that is, both the beauty and its fault-lines. Our brains need to come to grips with the different versions of the history of a country, depending on the chronicler of that history.

"This is particularly true for the country in which I have become a recent arrival. The original landscape has been substantially altered by the invasion of different colonisers, often to its detriment. It is an enduring pleasure to discover that some of the original inhabitants survive and care for land and the beautiful landscapes which survive despite these intrusions. The original inhabitants are also presenting the colonisers with a history that is much older and more refined than the history of conquest and subjugation.

"This work has been swirling around the dusty corners and various strata of abandoned old scenes and culture in the poet's mind, superimposing the 'double-edged' landscape and history of her current location."

<u>Note from Thea:</u>
Currawongs are three species of medium-sized passerine birds belonging to the genus Strepera in the family Artamidae native to Australia. These are the grey currawong, pied currawong, and black currawong. The common name comes from the call of the familiar pied currawong of eastern Australia and is onomatopoeic. (*Wikipedia.*)

[6] Thea Biesheuvel wrote this about her poem, 'Sermon on the Mound (of garbage)': "The topic suggested was that of *plastic.*
This evoked scenes seen during my travels, of mighty rivers coursing along with many little plastic bottles bobbing along on the waves, all discarded by those who preferred their water more refined than that available in its natural form, for good reasons, of course. There is so much unseen pollution of our waters as well as the visible proof that we don't care for our environment.

"I live in a village where the residents are church-going, god-fearing Christian people. Without in any way interfering with their preoccupations, my beliefs are that long ago, in a different land, the prophet told his followers to have 'dominion' over all living things and to take good care of them.

"We have recycling bins in our village where we are encouraged to take care of the environment by segregating our garbage into plastics and recyclable goods. It seldom happens. People can't be bothered. I am quite perturbed about that. This poem has been simmering away for quite some time.

"It resulted in an interspersing of descriptions of the damage we're inflicting with the preaching of the prophet as a contrast. It is in the hope that this message sinks in a little better than [do] the slogans we see exhorting us to buy ever more articles in plastic packages."

<u>Note from Thea</u>:
"Fancy" as in tapestry, sampler of embroidery, appliqué
work (*Roget's Thesaurus*)
 "Pong" as in stink, smell (*Collins Australian English
Dictionary*)

[7] Note from Liam:
"Stans": a slang term for crazed fans of a person or
celebrity

[8] Liam Blackford has supplied his English translation of the
two verses written in Chinese in his poem, 'Untitled 3', as
below. (In response to our question, Liam confirmed that
these are not quotations, but written by himself.—He speaks
and reads Chinese having studied for fifteen years.)

信息公得同步。
人民所接触的
成为所接受的。
充分控制信息、
把噪音弄清澈
是领导的责任。

Information and morality are synchronised.
What the people come in contact with
becomes what they accept.
Full control of information
and rendering noise into clarity
is a leader's responsibility.

我国所有道路
都归回到首都。
这里藏着势力
抢得翻天覆地。
长期以来如此，
也会永远依旧。

In our country,* all roads
lead to the capital.
Here is stored power
strong enough to flip heaven and earth.
It has been this way for a long time
and it shall be this way forever.

* 我国 *also commonly refers to China.*

Liam invites us to note that the content is written in metred verse in which each stanza has six lines and each line has six syllables. He comments, "This matches the overall poem in which there are six stanzas, each stanza has six lines and each line has six syllables."

Asked why he chose to include the two verses in Chinese, he replied, "The poem thematically touches on (amongst other things) Chinese governance and civilisation. Chinese works well in my metred form (the poem has six stanzas, each with six lines, each line with six syllables). Chinese idioms also permit complex meaning in a short space, such as 翻天覆地 (the earth and the sky turn upside down), which would have been hard to express in English while maintaining the metred form. It was a deliberate choice to use Chinese for two complete stanzas, and then to return to English. Importantly, the poem is dialogue-free and the poetic voice is unpersonified, which is maintained in both the English and the Chinese."

[9] Maria Elena Blanco describes how her poem, 'Waiting For Ulysses', came into existence. "It's funny: Inspiration. Some linguists now say it doesn't exist. Most poets no longer wait for it. I must admit that with all the horrible things going on in the world today, even in the realm of Nature, it *is* rather hard to find. It was certainly a lot easier for the Romantics: the Poet would just ride to a nearby lake, descend to its shore, lay bare the soul and be instantly enlightened with the glow of the right Words. Well, those times are gone. Not long ago, I found myself in an idyllic natural setting in the

south of Spain, aptly called Sirens' Reef. As I stood there surrounded by the magnificent landscape and the usual groups of people posing and chatting, I also took photos and photos were taken of me, which I then posted on my Facebook profile along with a brief caption alluding to the topics the place brought to mind: the Greek myths associated with the sirens, Homer's *Odyssey*, Ulysses. But not a line of verse, not a word came then to spark a poetic reaction to such spectacular images. A few days later, though, a dear poet friend responded from afar to my digital comment with the following question: "Would you like Ulysses if he did join you?" A dialogue ensued, and a suggestion on her part: "You could write a poem for him (with your reply perhaps) and submit it for the Proverse Poetry Prize 2019?" Thus springs Inspiration in the 21st century: from a remote Poet-to-Poet exchange through an electronic public medium in the elusive nature of cyberspace."

[10] Raymond Calbay writes, "Airports are about in-betweenness and lives in transit. The poem 'Nothing to declare' was inspired by a personal encounter with the breakdown of a baggage carousel while on holiday travel. It is a quiet reflection on how a temporary, plasticized territory sets us off to heights of ambivalence and wanderlust."

[11] Paola Caronni explains that her poem 'Arboreal Witness' was inspired by a big and beautiful tree planted in the centre of the garden of a hotel located on the banks of the Irrawaddy River in Bagan, Myanmar, where she stayed in 2014 and again in 2019.

"The large trunk and the long and winding branches of the lush tree gave away its old age and made me reflect on the past history of Myanmar, from the golden age of Bagan (when more than thirteen thousand temples, pagodas, and other religious structures were built) to the period of the repressive military rule in the country, to now. Hotel guests have been coming and going, but the tree has always been there to witness whatever happened under its branches, and in Myanmar. The appearance of a bride represents hope for a bright and prosperous future in this now fast-developing country."

<u>Note from Paola:</u>

'Lahpet' is the Burmese word for fermented or pickled tea. Myanmar is one of very few countries where tea is eaten as well as drunk. When tea leaves are harvested, the best of the crop is set aside for fermenting, while the rest is dried and processed for drinking tea. The freshly harvested tea leaves are briefly steamed, then packed into bamboo vats and set in pits, pressed by heavy weights for fermentation.

[12] Paola Caronni explains that, her poem, 'Restless Night', is a recollection of feelings and emotions which emerged when she woke up early after a restless summer night. The speaker is very alert and pays attention to what is happening around him/her. The sounds coming from outside the room trigger the longing for the familiar chirping of cicadas, not yet heard in the early morning. Memories resurface and take the reader to the speaker's childhood in his/her homeland, when life was still uncomplicated, and summertime was a happy season spent enjoying simple, repeated actions.

[13] Vincent Casaregola writes this about his poem, 'The Plastic Dead': "As a child, decades ago, I played at games of war with small plastic soldier figures. In an earlier era, these would have been made from tin or lead, but in the 1950s and 1960s, toy companies began to mold them from polyethylene and polystyrene. I enacted countless mock battles with these little figures, and when they died, they were but plastic toys, knocked over for a moment. Only later, as an adult, did I come to understand that our games of violence echo the very real violence of the larger world. My childhood insensitivity to the real horrors of war is not uncommon, and even today, children play war in the virtual worlds of computer and video games. I wrote the poem reflecting on how the rows of 'fallen' or 'dead' plastic toy soldiers could make us unconsciously accept war and its destruction as merely a game. We need to realize that, only

when we accept the concrete human costs of war, will we be able to find ways to maintain both peace and justice without unnecessary violence and death."

[14] Anne Casey writes the following about her poem, ''Either Way, The Fact Remains': "As a former environment journalist/author and mother, I worry greatly about the state of our precious planet and what we will leave behind for our children. Ecopolitics features large in my poetry, particularly in my second poetry collection, *out of emptied cups*, just published by Salmon Poetry. I often use statistics embedded in poems to emphasise key points—as is the case here.

"This 'reversal' poem interrogates the notion that the facts around human activity and the climate crisis remain the same: it is our attitude which needs to change. We need collective commitment to a universal response for there to be any progress towards a solution.

"Reading the poem in the standard way, from top to bottom, you find an extremely negative outlook—'the impact of human activities is irreversible' and Earth is hurtling towards certain destruction. However, when you reach the end, you are instructed to 'Now read each line from the bottom up', thereby finding the scenario is entirely reversed, and ending with the assertion that 'Every human heart has sufficient good at its core' to save this one and only Earth beneath our feet."

[15] Ian Chambers writes, "During a short vacation in the wilds of Donegal, I was struck by the world of the local farming people and what for me would have been a challenging existence in so many ways. Having Irish farm-labourer ancestors who lived through the Great Famine, I felt a strong empathy despite my own completely different life. This manifested itself in even the most innocuous aspects of the surroundings. I wanted to capture this feeling and take it home to enjoy and consider later. The fact that in the distance I could see Benbulben standing guard over the

grave of famed Irish poet W. B. Yeats strengthened that urge."

[16] Ian Chambers describes the situation that gave rise to his poem, 'For My 90th Birthday', as follows: "As I observed my mother's life in a care home it seemed to me that the residents had left their lives at the main entrance: they had been placed in a time capsule. Despite caring relatives and caring staff, they had somehow become a different species—one that had only a past."

[17] Of his poem, 'The Dying of the Light', Ian Chambers writes, "My mother's death, when it finally came, was quick. Although not unexpected, the timing had been unpredictable and unfortunately I was abroad. The first phone call from the duty nurse at the care home woke me in the early hours of the morning. For those few subsequent hours of helpless heartbeats and emotional attachment, lying in the dark waiting for the second call, it was almost as if I were once again in her womb."

[18] Ian Chambers writes this of his poem, 'Words': "When one thinks of powerful devices, particularly destructive ones, weapons and conflict spring to mind. But words are potentially the most powerful devices of all. Despite having zero mass they can travel vast distances even through the vacuum of space and survive for millennia in rocks, documents and now digital form. Words can bestow boundless individual happiness and optimism but they can equally lead to incomprehensible suffering and conflict."
<u>Note from Ian</u>:
Seanachaí: an Irish travelling storyteller who passes the "old lore" from generation to generation.

[19] Carl Flake Chapman explains, "When I learned that the theme of this year's poetry contest was 'plastics,' I immediately thought of the blue plastic tarps that are passed out to displaced people in places that have experienced devastation from either natural disasters or warfare. For me

they are the symbols of life that has been increasingly disrupted by natural or human causes.

"I had seen them in Dubrovnik, Croatia, when I arrived at the very end of the bombardment there that had devastated the beautiful old tile rooftops of the city that form a kind of carpet as you look across the city from the surrounding wall. And I had seen them on rooftops everywhere in the city of New Orleans when people were trapped in their houses by the flood that covered eighty percent of the city after Hurricane Katrina. They were also omnipresent in the aftermath of the worst wildfire in California history when the entire town of Paradise was burned to the ground. They are everywhere where there is disaster and displacement.

"As these events become more common, and as so many people are displaced from their homes, I fear that these blue tarps will also become more common."

[20] Fiona Chen writes: "Immersed in waves of ecstasy and tides of melancholy simultaneously, the author was in a mixed sentiment of opposing emotions when she wrote 'On One-Out-Of-The-Way Thing'. She had let her thought and eye roam and follow the embodiment of an unobtainable creature, leaving herself in constant doubt of her silent quest. She took her petty position as a drop of dew on a sunflower petal, whilst pledging its faith in a nightingale, who has neither tie nor obligation to the nameless droplet. Nevertheless, the impossible could always be realised through a little touch of imagination, which fortunately, is also what it finds so much joy in doing. It does not fear falling, nor does it fear the passing of time. It would willingly offer itself upon knowing the thirst of the nightingale.

"Clearly one should not live in a world built on unreal imagination, i.e. the 'out-of-the-way-thing', used with reference to *Alice's Adventures in Wonderland* by Lewis Carroll (Charles Lutwidge Dodgson). As the sun and moon merely get a glimpse of each other at dusk, the same is true of the droplet and the nightingale. Out-of-the-way things exist after all, if only 'upon pillars of hue'."

[21] Annie Christain explains "'Appearances" from *Criminal Cipher Code for Police Officers'*, as follows. "My poem was inspired by *Barnard's Universal Criminal Cipher Code* published in 1895. This book contains codes used by police to maintain secrecy in their internal telegrams. For my poem, I used slang of a dark or underground nature and imagined what each word's corresponding entry would be in a cipher code book. The collective entries provide enough details to give the reader hints that a shadowy, sinister meeting or bizarre ritual is taking place, but no exact specifics are given to clarify what is exactly happening or why. The way the entries are written also shows that those individuals attending the meeting would be speaking to each other in code and using books to decipher the words and/or relaying reports of the night to interested individuals, thus increasing tension and eeriness in the poem."

[22] Teresa Ngan-fung Chu writes that her, poem 'To Carry On', "was first drafted in 2011, mainly as a linguistic attempt to register the sense of weight and heaviness felt by the writer, who found the reality of life burdensome, and the business of living, exhausting."

She continues, "Evidently, with the writer drafting this back-story for Proverse in 2019, the writer has truly carried on and survived another eight years. During these years, as T.S. Eliot puts it so poetically, there has been time for 'a hundred visions and revisions'. Indeed, not only has the writer revised the original draft a few times in terms of both language and content; she is actually reading the poem in a different light as she writes this back-story.

"Now, she has a new vision. The poem is no longer about herself; instead, it is a story about her mother, who has been carrying on for even longer years, being eighty-seven years of age this year and still going strong.

"To carry on, one has to be strong. One has to be persevering. To carry on, one has to have faith, that eventually, something good will happen, to prove that all's well-worthy. To be able to carry on, one needs the Lord's kindest blessings.

"The dear 87-year-old lady to whom the poet owes her life, and so much more, has indeed carried on: living, loving and staying strong and faithful, despite setbacks and many challenges. The poet would like to dedicate this poem to her, to celebrate her strength, and her being the enduring and shining example of perseverance, service and selfless love.

"'A coffee a day keeps the burden at bay' is a lovely thought from a coffee company as part of its recent business promotion. How I love that formula. However, life over the years has told me that it would take more than a coffee a day to keep the burden at bay, just as it takes more than an apple a day to keep the doctor away.

"By the way, the 87-year-old lady, mother of the poet, needs no coffee, nor apple, daily. She just needs love, coming from God, and flowing from her to the world that continues, to life that goes on.

"So life goes on, as summed up by the clever Mr Robert Frost. So too I carry on…"

[23] Suzanne Cottrell explains that 'Mermaid Tears' (the title of her poem) is another name for sea glass, and continues: "I enjoy searching for and collecting sea glass that can be made into jewelry, as well as collecting interesting sea shells on North Carolina's beaches. In order for a fragment of glass to become smooth and frosted, it tumbles in the surf for at least seven to ten years. The best opportunities to locate sea glass are after high tide two to three days after a storm. Sea glass is more difficult to find with the increased use of plastics and the recycling of glass bottles and jars.

"According to legend, sea glass became known as mermaid tears after a mermaid angered Neptune, God of the Sea. She calmed strong winds and turbulent waves in order to save a ship's captain with whom she had fallen in love. Neptune banished the mermaid to the depths of the ocean for interfering with the forces of nature. Her tears, sea glass, continue to wash up on shores around the world."

Notes from Suzanne:

"'Lilliputian' means very small and is referenced in the novel, *Gulliver's Travels*, by Jonathan Swift. Swift created the country of Lilliput, in which everything is tiny."

"Emerald Isle is a North Carolina town on the western end of Bogue Banks, a barrier island located between Bogue Sound and the Atlantic Ocean. The confluence of the North bound, warm Gulf Stream Current and the South bound, cold Labrador or Artic Current off Cape Hatteras causes shifting sand bars which make the waters difficult to navigate. These waters off the outer banks of North Carolina are referred to as the Graveyard of the Atlantic. Over 600 shipwrecks have been discovered."

[24] Stéphane D'Amour's poem, 'A Memory', was written, she tells us, "shortly after a visit at a Sophie Calle exhibition in Montréal. "As I entered a large room filled with a dozen huge screens hanging from the ceiling, each one showing a video, telling a slow-paced story, I was enigmatically drawn by a woman turning her back to the camera while looking at the sea (were her eyes open?). I left the screen before the end of the story, and never saw her face. (Did she turn around?)"

[25] Helen Davis explains that, "'The Sog' is really my mum's name for a fleeting depression, coming and going but always around. A bit like the rain in Carmarthen, my home town in Wales. You can be in a sog or have a sog. In both cases the 'Sog' will lift."

[26] Lawdenmarc Decamora writes this: "**plasticine ιδέες**—or the musically stylized Bacharach-like composition of ideas through structural fragmentation, dissonance, colour and plasticity—deconstructs the individual's Romantic fascination with 'bridges' or the grammaticality of beauty that only connects cultural identity to the dialogic necessity of the epic consciousness of literature monumentalizing itself into an aesthetic or belletristic spectacle of the page— itself an elegant presentation of memory rather than the

sublime foregrounding of the realistic account of history and truth, the often untouched narrative of forgetting in peacetime. Moreover, the stereographic plurality or plasticity of ιδέες (Greek for 'ideas') can resuscitate creative production that almost always stagnates, as it were, in a stasis of material conditions.

"This poem therefore aims to 'de-Romanticize' bridges or its pronounced aesthetic banality/structural linearity by means of confronting the mysterious, the grotesque, or simply the racing 'tunnels' engaging life in the inside-outside critical core of human experience as well as contextual associations often rationalized through and by the 'unstructurality of play'—say, the allusion to Alfred Kreymborg's radical little magazine *Others* translated as 'Kreymborg flowers' in the poem, the articulate reference to Ezra Pound's *Make it New!* as indubitably the poem's central theme, not to mention T.S. Eliot's oeuvre pushing for impersonal poetics, and my polychromatic response to 'plasticine porters' in the Beatles song *Lucy in the Sky with Diamonds*.

"Ideas in **plasticine ιδέες** follow the Barthesian model, constructed and completed as what I used to call 'tunnels.' These seemingly syntactic tunnels travel through one's literary imagination or heterotopic dreamscapes, and while the poem inspires these rhizomic tunnels to navigate the abysmal 'meta-spectacle' of gesture, language or moment of poem*ness*, the mind like the many-coloured jeepneys of Manila, where driving past roast goose restaurants in Shek Kip Mei or spotting stilt houses in Kampong Kleang, attempt to explore the transgeneric textualities of the everyday, alongside the unstructurality of time and space, the littoral and the liminal.

[27] Neil Douglas comments that in four separate poems, he has written, in turn, about, an eclipse, an assassination, a courtship and a leaving., observing that, "at first glance there may not seem to be a connection but all the poems deal with relationships and emotions of different kinds played out against a back drop of the natural world."

As for his fifth poem, 'Nan Lian Garden', he tells us that this, "was written after a visit to this beautiful Hong Kong park in 2019. It brings together some of the themes of the other poems but it is primarily about the tension between Humanity and Nature, the making and breaking of rules and the uneasy friction between conformity and freedom. It is a poem for the times in which we live."
Note from Neil:
"Mire dromble": Old English name for a male bittern.

28 Jennifer Eagleton writes that 'Blue Mondays' was inspired by reading an article about "blue Mondays"—a name given to a day in January that claimed to be the most depressing day of the year as calculated by a travel company which claimed to have found the date by using an algorithm. Humans try to find their "own" algorithm, and thus their own "nature" through the use of scientific fitness devices.

29 Ahmed Elbeshlawy tells us that his poem, 'A Call from the Well', was written for Jamal Khashoggi. On October 2nd 2018, the Saudi journalist, Jamal Khashoggi, entered the consulate of his own country in Istanbul to obtain documents in order to get married. He was murdered and dismembered inside the consulate by an assassination squad believed by some to be sent by the Saudi Crown Prince. His body has never been found. The media have put out many speculative scenarios about where his body parts could have been disposed of. In one such speculative scenario, it has been suggested that the assassins disposed of Jamal's body parts in a well in the back yard of the Saudi Consul-General's residence in Istanbul.

30 Ahmed Elbeshlawy wrote, 'The Message of the Music', in 2003, after listening to Schubert's *String Quartet in D Minor, Death and the Maiden* in Hong Kong's City Hall. He tells us that, "My reception of the musical performance … was significantly affected by Roman Polanski's film *Death and the Maiden* which I saw some time previously.

"In Polanski's film, Schubert's *Quartet* is a central motif. It backgrounds the heroine's memory of her ordeal in a dictatorial régime's prison in which she was tortured and raped by a doctor who played Schubert's *Death and the Maiden* while raping her.

In City Hall, there was indeed a remarkable girl with bushy flaxen hair in the audience and I kept gazing at it from time to time. For a moment, I imagined that I may not be that different from the apparently civilized music-loving doctor, listening attentively like everyone else to the music, while concealing the most perverse and dangerous thoughts."

[31] Ahmed Elbeshlawy tells us that his poem, '21st Century Immigrant', "was inspired by two pieces of recurring news; the ordeal of illegal immigrants on their way from their countries to the developed world and the pollution of the sea by plastic refuse. In its latest reports, the UN refugee agency said that the proportion of those losing their lives while trying to cross the Mediterranean to Europe has risen so sharply that 1,095 people died at sea just between January and July 2019, amounting to one death for every 18 arrivals. In June alone, the proportion hit one death for every seven arrivals. At the same time, it is estimated that 1.15 to 2.41 million tons of plastic trash enter the ocean each year. The BBC says that the equivalent of a truck full of plastic is emptied into the world's oceans every single minute. The poem was written on Anglers' Beach in Hong Kong during the summer of 2019. Every summer, the beach becomes so infested with refuse from the sea that it becomes unthinkable to enter the water."

[32] Rayn Epremian writes, "I wrote 'All-Inclusive Guilt-Trip Getaway' in a damp notebook on a beach on Isla Mujeres, Mexico. I was enjoying the oddity of a luxury holiday with three of my oldest friends, thanks to one of them being gifted a free-of-charge stay at the resort. Unused to such easy ubiquity, we accepted free piña-coladas to the point of dehydration and marveled at the colours of the sea during

another stunning sunset. A cruise ship on the horizon, full of folks headed to Cancun for a similar experience, spouted haze into the sherbet-striped sky. I was grateful for my good fortune, the good company of my friends, and the good food that I could not actually afford. But watching that smoke rise reminded me that 'included' is never the same as 'free': these luxuries all came at a cost, even if I wasn't going to have to foot the bill thanks to my friend's freebie. Not all things are paid for with money. The human desire for decadence and the value, monetary or otherwise, that we place on such comforts is part of a culture that contributes to the depletion of natural resources, the pollution of the world's waters, and the destruction of our fellow creatures' habitats. And, of course, luxury tourism, like all kinds of consumption, benefits one group of humans at a cost to others. Unable to ignore this reality, even on the beach, I wrote this poem."

[33] Kate Hawkins writes, "'Takeaway Eaters' is a haiku based on this year's anthology theme—plastic. The poem's aim is to allow the reader to consider the world's reliance on single-use plastic and the damage this causes our fragile ecosystems. In wake of the 2019 worldwide Climate Marches, I feel more than ever that poetry can help us examine the areas we all need to improve."

[34] Aiden Heung writes that his poem, 'A Stranger On The Street', is about a beggar who once lived beneath an overpass in the city of Shanghai. "I used to see him on my way back from work. I can't help thinking of him every time now as I walk by the empty lot. I'm not different from him, being one of many insignificant lives who strive to make a living in this metropolis. I wish I had my life in control, but I'm, like many, a tiny peg to a colossal machine. Any whimsical 'twist of plot' will cost me the chance to a 'decent' life. The beggar might just be another victim of such a case, which does not mean he doesn't deserve respect or compassion. But the fact is, such respect and compassion are generally lacking in a society dominated by the desire

for money and power; more often than not, these beggars are driven away by force because their presence is already inimical to the 'integrity' of the city. The fair treatment of the less fortunate is in urgent need. It's a writer's responsibility to tell, and if he somehow succeeds in invoking thoughts, to bring such a change to society."

[35] Of his poem, 'At Dragon's Back, Hong Kong', Aiden Heung writes: "Dragon's Back is my favorite hiking route in Hongkong, a city I always love and support. When you come to To Tei Wan, first head down-hill to a small beach where the sea spreads like blue velvet in front of you. The wind brings an exotic and sweet smell, like over-ripe orange mixed with mint. Then you follow the flights of stairs back to the beginning. The steepness might be thwarting; the sun might be overwhelmingly hot; gravity pulls at your feet, ready to diminish you to something weightless, perhaps a shadow. The humid air gnaws on your skin like termites; the path is tortuous, you have no idea where it might take you but you know you are on the right track. It is not an easy trek. When you almost want to give up, suddenly, space opens up, as if a new world suddenly took shape, before that, you were just slumbering in a heavy dream. You are standing now on the ridge, on your left and right is the velvet sea again which blends now into the endless sky beneath which small islands are studded like green peridots. In front, the path suddenly loses its harsh intimidation and gallops into a tapestry of rocks, bushes and visiting seagulls. Suddenly, you feel free, never so free and you want to stay free forever. You now understand where the sweat-drenched road beneath your feet will take you."

[36] Aiden Heung explains that his poem, 'Salvation', is a record of an experience. "I visited a small temple on the north bund of Shanghai. It was, like almost all temples in China, also a tourist attraction where you had to pay to enter. There was the grandiose temple gate, a few guards dressed in quite a slovenly manner but who certainly had the attitude of the four angry deities who safeguarded

the 'heavenly gate'. In the rising incense smoke (of course you are welcome to buy incense), the whole temple area seemed too garish to be true, as if those who sat on the podium were old-time mandarins, not deities. This poem was not written against Buddhism as a religion, but written as irony, a slight reproach to the commercialized way the belief is organized on nowadays. I didn't go in after all."
Note from Aiden:
 "Heavenly gate", is a direct translation from the Chinese word, 天门.

[37] Elmira / Carrie Hooper writes that her three poems were all written during April National Poetry Month, and were partly inspired by some of the daily prompts sent out that month by Alice Massa, a member of Behind Our Eyes, a writers group for people with disabilities, to which Elmira, who is totally blind, belongs. "On the first day of National Poetry Month, she suggested we write a poem with the word 'whisper' either in the title or in the poem itself. That day, as I was coming home from work, I felt a gentle breeze that seemed to whisper. That experience, along with Alice's prompt, inspired the poem, 'The Whispering Wind's Serenade.'"

The suggestion to write a poem in which skyscrapers were used as a metaphor inspired, 'How to Build a Living Skyscraper.'

"Another prompt was to write a poem of comfort. A friend of mine was going through a stressful period. I wanted to offer her some words of encouragement, and Alice's prompt provided the perfect opportunity to do that. I wrote 'Peace Offering' and sent it to my friend. She appreciated it very much."

[38] R. J. Keeler gives a detailed description of how his poem 'Invasive Species', came into the form published here: "During the summer of 2016, I employed a male college student for a few weeks to help me dig a 2"-deep ditch around the foundation of my old house so that I could lay in a foundation-footing drain.

"The poem actually began on 3/27/2017 when the word 'legerdemain' came into my consciousness as I was writing in my daily journal. Quite a lot of the poem was written right then and there, that same day, according to my journal notes. The first written version of the poem, on 3/27, contained the first two stanzas pretty much complete. This first version also contained the lyrics to the Dobie Gray song beginning, 'Oh, give me the beat, boys, and free my soul'.

"Two days later, on the 29th, I attended a lecture titled 'Dark Times' on the topic of myth, which mentioned, among other items, that 'stories are vessels to contain things we can't understand,' that 'no one is ever really alone in the world,' and other relevant things.

"I continued to free-associate and do online research over the next two days and to make more notes, which contained … [the following] references among many others:

- "fetishizes the skree
- "The origin of consciousness in the breakdown of the bicameral mind" (I did not explicitly use this theme in the poem but the concept of *division* was introduced)
- "An article from Wikipedia, "The evolutionary impact of invasive species" (*which results in a highly successful species that is altering the composition and function of the native communities it invades*)
- "Another article from Wikipedia, "The Indirect Evolutionary Consequences of Mixing" (*In any ecosystem there is a web of interaction among the biotic components of differing specificities*)

"The second rough draft of the poem around the 29th contained all four stanzas almost complete. Since it was written, there have been thirteen separate revisions to this poem."

[39] Zachary Knox comments about his poem, 'A Monolith to Demeter'. "It simply was me tapping into males' deeply internalized guilt for the plunder of the earth in the name of

progress. We have forgotten our connection to the feminine as a result and thus forgotten how to heal the wounds."

[40] Lynda Lambert explains, "I wrote 'Anticipated Arrival of a Predicted Blizzard' in the winter season. The television and radio stations were telling the public that a large blizzard was coming so that people could be prepared. When this happens, people rush to the local grocery store and stand in the checkout lines with their shopping carts full of groceries. It seems to be something that is an over-response to the announcement that a storm is coming, for it is winter and such storms are normal here in western Pennsylvania in the USA. Even if it is a really bad storm, it's not typical for the stores to be closed because of it. I was imagining all of the things I would get at the store if I actually went there and how it would feel and look. I imagined my husband and myself standing in the long check-out line, glancing out the windows, and talking about our fears."

[41] Lynda Lambert comments on her poems, 'Hades Song', and, 'Persephone's Song', at the same time. "In the two poems each person is expressing their own story of a crime that took place in a field of wild flowers one day as described in the Ancient History of mythology. As I worked on the poems, I could hear each of them telling their side of the story—How the crime was committed, and why, and the aftermath of it. I felt as if I was hearing a duet performance on a stage. It was as though I was in the audience listening to the inner dialogue of each of them. And, I felt compassion for them as each expressed their emotions and thoughts."

[42] Susan Lavender gives the following background to, 'Spill Those Beans!': "My life has been difficult. I am not an optimist but I like to think I am a realist rather than a pessimist. Especially at times when I am not involved in theatre—acting is the only thing I love doing—I depend on coffee to get me through the day.

"Granted: drinking coffee is an addiction but it is surely also a life saver. Switzerland has stockpiled coffee since the inter-bellum years between the world wars, together with other staples necessary for human and animal survival, in case of shortages caused by war or natural disasters. In the spring of 2019, however, Switzerland announced tentative plans to end its emergency coffee reserves by the end of 2020 on the basis that, having practically no calories, coffee is *not essential to life*. How can that be when some of us, who are not buoyed by a natural enthusiasm for life, would never get out of bed in the morning without it?"

[43] Iris Litt writes, "My poem, 'Plastika', had been in my mind ever since a trip to Greece. The entire experience in the poem was still vivid. When I saw your request for poems on plastics, it all clicked, and I wrote and edited the poem."

[44] Brittany Mishra writes about 'And Then Eve': "I wanted to write a modern creation story that showed Eve's realization of her own autonomy and limitations in a body and a world created by God. At the end, Eve notices God is afraid of her when she bites back. In turn, God realizes his foolishness and arrogance for creating a being that could destroy and outnumber him. Ultimately, creation is about power and control. What happens when the created overturns the creator?"

[45] Helen Oliver explains the background to her poem, 'Nuclear ponderings—forgotten victims', as follows: "In 1976 I joined Sailing Vessel (SV) *Fri* in Hong Kong, volunteering for Greenpeace New Zealand. On this voyage, SV *Fri*'s mission was two-fold. First, to raise awareness of the proliferation of nuclear weapons, given that a number of countries were by then testing and developing nuclear arsenals. Second, to publicise the dangers of nuclear testing by drawing attention to the problems caused both in Micronesia, which SV *Fri* had recently visited (from 1946 to 1958, the US used Bikini Atoll in the Marshall Islands as their test site; the radioactive fallout especially affected the

coral atol of Rongelap) and in Polynesia (from 1966 to 1996, Mururoa Atoll was used for French nuclear testing, first atmospheric and then underground).

"In 1973, a flotilla of private boats, including SV *Fri*, sailed north to the French testing zone. They were joined by two New Zealand Navy frigates, which indicated the strength of New Zealand's opposition to atmospheric testing. Beginning in 1974, SV *Fri* embarked on a 3-year epic 40,233 kilometers 'Pacific Peace Odyssey' voyage, carrying the peace message to all nuclear states around the world

"I wrote this poem after reading current reports detailing the devastating legacy of US and French nuclear testing for the forgotten victims, whose lives have been so significantly blighted."

<u>Notes from Helen:</u>
jellyfish babies is the name given to babies born with no bones (due to radiation poisoning) who die soon after birth.
Manus, Christmas Island and Nauru refer to detention centres set up by the Australian government to prevent boat people reaching Australia and gaining refugee status.

Sources (just a few of many):
https://newsarchive.ohchr.org/EN/NewsEvents/Pages/Displa yNews.aspx?NewsID=12025&LangID=E
https://www.washingtonpost.com/sf/national/2015/11/27/a-ground-zero-forgotten/?utm_term=.324ba16bc888
https://www.rnz.co.nz/international/pacific-news/394585/call-for-us-to-do-more-to-address-nuclear-legacy-in-marshall-islands?fbclid=IwAR0q-N3Ue0lJm5-mS0HBCg-pvHTgxYo7OJTkdyQU_u9G1RI53vMhE6qQxXE
https://www.rnz.co.nz/international/pacific-news/391104/two-more-cancers-recognised-over-french-nuclear-tests

[46] Writing of her poem, 'Seashore', Patience O'Neill explains, "The country of my birth, Britain, is an island, so

it is surrounded by the sea, and therefore also surrounded by a variety of sea shores. The sea and seashores have always been a source of great inspiration for writers and for artists, who are fascinated by the changing seasons and the moods that the sea shore can evoke. For example, on the East coast, Norfolk and Suffolk, the land is very flat, as is the sea shore, so when the tide is out, there is a vast expanse of beach. On the South West coast, Cornwall, the coast line has steep dramatic rocks and wild seas. Beachcombing, the theme of my poem, literally means combing or sifting found objects on the beach, as you walk along. It is a hobby, carried out as a solo activity, that people can find meditational, because they are listening to the sea and gazing at the beach to see what they can find., usually a mixture of natural and man-made objects which have been smoothed by the waves of the sea. Some beachcombers use these found objects to decorate their gardens or to make sculptures or wind chimes."

[47] Of her poem, 'Gentleness', Rena Ong writes: "I think many of us go through life balancing our commitments and often health issues so that we present ourselves to others in a form that THEY can cope with. Presenting a face of bravery, positive demeanor and inner strength, though good aims in themselves, we are really feeling as though we are continually tight-rope walking through life's balancing act.

"From a woman's view point in this generation where we are expected, as women, to be warriors, strong, '60 is the new 40'; when many are actually quiet souls, who enjoy their quiet life but are made to feel guilty for not continually pushing themselves, yet at the same time told to be content, be thinner, be tougher, do more; or perhaps have chronic health issues that are not readily noticed, thus cannot keep up with this unrealistic ideal due to exhaustion or pain, I felt that someone needed to point out that 'good enough' is enough. To show understanding that people do not think the way the media portrays, in other words…. Be gentle to one another."

[48] Of her poem, 'Lullaby for a man' Rena Ong writes: "This is a poem, of which there are many, of how I feel towards my son who is now a grown man and lives abroad. That the feeling of love and protection I have had for him since he was born remains the same, will never die and most important that he knows on paper, which he can hold in his hands and touch when life happens, that he is always loved. As I truly believe love never dies, 'always' is also how I sign my letters to both him and my husband. Love is always."

[49] Rena Ong writes that her poem, 'Silence', "for me is multi-layered and comes from observing both marginalized groups—youth and individuals whose ideas and feelings, which could begin resolution, understanding, new paths or amazing creativity—are ignored and instead they become despondent and lonely and at worse bitter and vengeful.

"The birds circling the air in 'murmuration' is there to show the myriad of thoughts that swirl in an individual's head that are pressing to get out and be heard, but when ignored, as with the bird's flight, soon dissipates and is seen no more."

[50] In relation to his poem, 'Merri Creek—Brunswick East, Melbourne', Martin Jon Porter writes, "The Merri Creek is a suburban waterway that flows through parts of Melbourne, Australia. It's a place I frequent on lunch breaks and seek momentary refuge from the grind of city life. My poem observes the early indicators of its mistreatment, and what might eventuate if this continues."

[51] Of, 'Remembering Snow', Joanna Radwanska Williams writes: "Climate change is producing not only global warming but unusually cold weather as well. Watching the news of an extreme cold spell in North America, I saw a beautiful image of the frozen Niagara falls. Suddenly I felt nostalgic for my childhood in Poland, when experiencing snow was not an unusual event. Since I now live in Macau, snow is but a fond memory."

[52] Joanna Radwanska-Williams comments on, 'The Life Cycle Of A Beach Ball': "This poem was inspired by this year's theme, 'Plastic'. Playing with a beach ball is such a joyful, carefree pastime. But if the beach ball gets swept up by the waves and lost at sea, eventually it disintegrates and becomes 'microplastic' and 'nanoplastic', and permanently enters the global food chain. The long-term consequences are detrimental to all living beings."

[53] Joanna Radwanska-Williams writes this about, 'The Pendant': "As a jewel, coral is so beautiful! Seeing an exhibition of coral jewelry in Taipei, I felt entranced. And yet the coral spoke to me of the whole process of its transformation from the exoskeleton of a living creature to a human artifact. The process highlights the coral's beauty, but harms its existence in nature, because coral is being fished out or 'mined' from the sea."

[54] C.N. Rajalakshmi writes this about the poem, 'Fresh Start': "A person sensitive to nature and human relationships, can't but poetically witness the leaves in the fall, the blossoms in the spring, all bringing with them a change and a forestaste of things to come.
These beauteous forms add colours to life, reiterating the philosophy of wheeling it over."

[55] C.N. Rajalakshmi explains that the poem, 'Vishnu, The Preserver And Protector', was inspired by the vibration and ambience of prayers.
Notes by C.N. Rajalakshmi:
Lord Vishnu: An Indian God. According to Indian scriptures and religious texts he is the protector and preserver of the whole universe.
Aadi Sesha: King of Snakes according to Indian scriptures and religious texts, Lord Vishnu is resting on coils of this serpent.
Atman: The 'Self 'or the 'Soul'

[56] Harsh Ramchandani writes this about his poem, 'From the rooftop': "I was inspired to write this poem after spending an early evening on my building's rooftop. I don't usually spend time up there in the summer, but a friend had recently introduced me to pipe-smoking and that gave me an excuse to step out of the apartment. I live in a busy Kowloon district and the crowded streets around me are often a source of frustration with its noise and excessive lighting. On this occasion though, I was feeling relaxed and was inspired by the change in perspective. The sound of construction, traffic and people that typically would frustrate me, gave life to the city. The view of old and new buildings with their lights spilling onto each other, combined with the distant view of mountains, brought out the city's vibrance and character. This poem was my attempt at capturing that. Though I was on my own at the time I mentioned in the poem that 'we remain at peace'. In this case 'we' doesn't refer to anyone in particular. I felt that the experience was better shared and would like to think that in a city of seven million people, there were others that found themselves in a similar situation that evening.

[57] Patrick Reardon explains that his poem, 'Myrrh' is a meditation on treasures and the loss of treasures, including the treasures bestowed to Jesus by the Magi (and later used after crucifixion), the treasure of $100 given to Jurgis in Upton Sinclair's novel *The Jungle*, the envisioned treasures of heaven, and, most of all, the treasure of life, which, unlike heaven, is here to be savoured or fled.
<u>Note from Patrick</u>:
"pols": politicians

[58] Vinni Relwani writes, "I was deeply affected by the 2019 mass shootings in places of worship in different parts of the world. In the aftermath of each of these events, such sadness. In the penning of 'The Walls Cried', I found an expression for my sorrow."

[59] Angelo Rizzi tells us, "I wrote these two poems ('Change' and 'No man's land') a few years ago. The theme is hope, the hope for a change, a change of the situation in which I found myself, for I lived as if in a trap. Had I fallen into a trap, or had I put myself in this trap all by myself? I asked help from poetry and rather ironically, I came out of it: a winner.

[60] Aparna Upadhyaya Sanyal writes as follows about, 'A Confession of Appetite': "This poem is so deeply personal, it's difficult for me to write about it in language that is not verse. For verse is my saviour and safe space that lets me express the emotions I normally hide from myself. This poem speaks of a time in my early life when I struggled with an eating disorder and so much more. I was broken: all jagged pieces inside. To say that I did not like myself is an understatement. My feelings of worthlessness were all enveloping. Now, as a functional and mostly-healed adult and mother to a six-year-old, I find myself trying to seek healing through nurturing my son."

[61] Of, 'Early Larger-than-life' Memories', Aparna Upadhyaya Sanyal writes: "My grandparents were an institution: 'grand' in every sense of the word. We, their grandchildren, viewed them with awe and sometimes fear. Growing up, they were not accessible, to our childish minds—it always felt like they were engaged in big, larger-than-life pursuits. We spent entire summers in their home, observing them, learning lessons we would not realise we had learnt until decades later. They were such strong personalities and clashed against each other with a roughness and tenacity that confounded our young minds. They were overwhelming and overpowering in their love, in their ambitions and in the lives they lived. I think of them everyday now that they are gone and remember the little things—those that crept away from my child-memory, and that come back to me in grown-up dreams every night."
Notes from Aparna Upadhyaya Sanyal:
Nani: Grandmother in Hindi

Nanaji: Grandfather in Hindi
Ghalib: one of the pen-names of Mirza Asadullah Baig
Khan (1797 –1869), a
prominent Urdu and Persian poet during the last years of
the Mughal Empire. See
<https://en.m.wikipedia.org/wiki/Ghalib>.
Mir Taqi Mir: Mir Muhammad Taqi Mir (1723 – 1810),
an Urdu poet of Mughal India. His pen-name was, "Mir":
See <https://en.m.wikipedia.org/wiki/Mir_Taqi_Mir/>.

[62] Aparna Upadhyaya Sanyal writes about, 'Grouted into
Those Tiles', as follows: "Trying to surface from an abusive
relationship is never easy, and writing this poem helped me
deal with some of that emotional baggage. I would lock
myself in bathroom stalls, staring at the tiles to try and make
some sense of my situation. There are many ways in which I
coped with that situation. This poem tries to put words to
overwhelming memories of a turbulent time."

[63] Of, 'Whispering the Family Tree to my Son at Night',
Aparna Upadhyaya Sanyal writes: "It is difficult to write
intimately about one's family and its history, without feeling
as if you are betraying them and dishonouring their
memories. Poetry is my safe space in which I express my
deepest fears without feeling overwhelmed by them. The
hereditary nature of insanity plays on my mind every day as
my partner and I try to build a stable, loving home for our
child. I hope in his case that nurture wins over nature and
that he is able to carry into adulthood a strong sense of
peace and love. I hope that I am able to distill the values that
lie at the core of my familial memories faithfully and that he
can view his ancestry with a critical yet non-judgemental
eye."
Notes from Aparna Upadhyaya Sanyal:
Daadi: Fraternal grandmother
Par-daadi: Great grandmother (fraternal)
Nahi: 'No' in Hindi
Par-naani: Great grandmother (maternal)

^{64} 'Bending into Blue' was written in response to a painting by Sarah Yeoman called "Cabin Dreams."

^{65} 'The Flowing' is about Allegra Jostad Silberstein's, "interest in shadows and the unknown in this wonder of our life here on earth."

^{66} Hayley Solomon writes of, 'Plastic Promise': "This somewhat surreal poem looks at the liquidity of the dream state, so elusive, yet poignantly meaningful at one and the same time. Dreams work in synchrony with our consciousness, but in direct antagonism to our logic. We perceive, but in a manner that is dissonant with our cognition. It is my contention that this peripheral processing of ideas, images, perceptions, is psychologically important but as difficult to annotate or capture as rainbows or moonbeams. I have incorporated the concept of plastic, here, in the sense of both elasticity and falsehood. A dream trembles on a promise then recedes, it gives the truth then snatches it away, effectively acting as an elastic falsehood, or a 'plastic'—as opposed to 'authentic'—promise."

^{67} Hayley Solomon writes of her poem, 'Butterfly Effect': "I wrote this poem wishing to rip asunder beauty, exposing the harshness of our willful self destruction. For this reason, I began the poem prettily, in a lyrical, poetic, quasi-classical style, changing course with the flap of the butterfly wings and the philosophical introduction of the concept of consequence. There, is, of course, religious allusion—both in the phrase 'we know not what we did' and in the ultimate deification of plastic, a modern form of idolatry. My language, though still liberal in the use of assonance, and alliteration, is harsh—there is a movement from stylized rhyme to no rhyme at all, or only the veriest echoes, denoting consequence and chaos. Cadent vestiges of lost harmony are heard through the occasional rhyming echo. I end with irony. While man faces mortality, the god he has created—vile plastic—will progress to an ignominious immortality. The phrase 'Thrones of junk' provides a stark

contrast to 'so soft the sound, so simple, soft and sweet'—
nothing is beautiful anymore. The poem is intended as a
warning—every action we take has a consequence, every
moment of inattention, of lack of caring, has monumental
flow on effect for generations."
<u>Note from Hayley</u>:
In chaos theory, the *butterfly effect* is the sensitive
dependence on initial conditions in which a small change in
one state of a deterministic nonlinear system can result in
large differences in a later state.
See <u>https://en.wikipedia.org/wiki/Butterfly_effect</u>

[68] Hayley Ann Solomon explains that her poem, 'Whose
fault is that?' is written in a quasi haiku style, capturing
fragments of feeling, a sense of nostalgia and regret, the
nuance of unrealised potential, of momentary effervescence
in an eternity of half light.

She continues, "Plastic *is* that. Humans have created it
for a few thoughtless seconds of utility and have ignored the
immensity of its harmfulness against the backdrop of time.
I have taken an unusual position of slight pity for plastic. If
plastic were sentient, it would have cause to feel jaded, ill-
used and abused. Created for futile longevity, it is never
afforded the dignity of retirement, of sweet disintegration
back to the elements.

"Through man's carelessly ingenious pursuit of
utility—however fleeting the need—plastic is forced to exist
forever. It will eventually be discarded, then evolve to
become a killer, a strangler of oceans. Plastic is doomed to
become jettisoned flotsam—forgotten, but nevertheless
potently—and patently—destructive.

"The last line, the rhetorical question, 'Whose fault is
that?', is designed to cast blame where it belongs and
highlights the absolute point of this poem."

[69] Abbie Taylor explains: "During a meeting of my monthly
poetry group, it was suggested that we each write a poem in
the form of a prayer. Having lost parents, grandparents, and
a husband, I developed the idea to write a poem in which I

prayed to whatever being resides above, if there is one, asking that being to reach out to my lost loved ones and tell them that I still miss them and look forward to being reunited with them. Since I'm not a believer in prayer, I decided to make the poem brief by creating an acrostic that spells out the word "prayer." I don't know if it's possible to join loved ones after you die. I can only hope."

[70] Of her poem, 'A Plastic Made Treasure', Luisa Ternau writes, "Nowadays plastic is normally shown as something to avoid or to find a more recyclable substitute for. This poem would like to be a humorous reminder of the origin of plastic as a substitute for costly materials. Thus the little girl is happy with a doll whose features look similar to those of an unaffordable bisque doll and, even better, cannot break as easily!"

[71] Luisa Ternau explains that, 'A Time of Life' is a sombre musing on a time of life when illness strikes and there is little hope of recovery. Life seems to go out of one's body in the same way that a medicine bottle is emptied: drop by drop. Sooner such intensity of life will be forgotten by all. A sense of uselessness could prevail. This feeling is avoided by the presence of dreams, with which everyone falls in love, openly, so that life can be filled by their presence and continue.

[72] Of her poem, 'Out of Their Cage'. Luisa Ternau writes: "The human condition is navigating in uncertainty. Freedom looks at hand and yet it seems too difficult to attain, even to dream of. Therefore the newly uncaged birds prefer to move back inside the meagre comfort of their cage. There they will remain with their vague dreams of a better condition which does not seem to be in view for them."

[73] Luisa Ternau explains that, 'Seaside Lullaby,' "is a lullaby to innocence. The little child of the sea represents innocence with its seemingly impossible existence in this world."

[74] Of her poem, 'The Voice', Luisa Ternau writes that it, "ponders over what will remain of this palpable life in the far future. Only a voice! But someone will still recognize and cherish it."

[75] Ed Tiesse writes: "In the summer, we often walk early on Sunday morning before most people are up and about. I was inspired by the early morning air before the humidity engulfs Chicago. The morning light and the lone piano playing was for me a near religious experience."

[76] Deepa Vanjani writes that her poem 'The Mask-Maker's Bian Lian' is, "a gentle reminder to all of us of the human species that the virtue of being human reigns above all. If one has the wisdom to acknowledge this truth, all riches and ambitions shrink into insignificance."

She continues, "During my visit to Hong Kong in 2018 I happened to read a magazine which had an article on the ancient Chinese art of Bian Lian. I was struck by the idea, and when writing the poem the word came back to me as it resonated with the theme of the poem.

"I have set the poem in the bygone era, and have therefore used words like 'sire'. There is the typically old Indian or Middle East kind bazaar i.e. market place where the mask-maker sits selling his wares.

"Humility and dropping of ego have a great value put on them in the Indian tradition, for both open up doors of our soul's awakening into a new realm."

Note from Deepa:
Bian Lian: the traditional Chinese art used in operas translated as "Face Changing". I read an article on it in a magazine during my visit to Hong Kong in 2018.

[77] Peter Verbica writes, "Book clubs invite us to read works outside our normal orbits of interest; such a gathering is singularly to blame for my reading the apocryphal *Book of*

Enoch, referenced in *The Dead Sea Scrolls*. The prophet imagines fallen angels mating with earthlings who in turn give birth to giants. If you enjoy the poem, 'From the Scent of Trees,' you have the imaginative and troubled prophet Enoch to thank for its genesis."

[78] George Watt explains that, "Usually the Aristotean concept of anagnorisis is applied to narrative, either in fiction or on the stage, to describe an important moment of realisation which the protagonist undergoes. He or she senses or discovers something of truth in the moment either of psychological insight or some essence in the wider world. Using the concept as the poem's title, points to the suggestion that the concept can also be used to approach what is happening in any short lyric of personal discovery."

[79] George Watt explains that his poem, 'By a river in Zhejiang Province pondering the end of the world', "is a whimsical view of an ecological crisis. While at an international conference in China my colleagues and I were advised to visit a historic row of shop houses that ran alongside a fast flowing river. But on arrival at the site, interest in the architecture and history and culture immediately palled in view of the river which was carrying a vast quantity of plastic and polystyrene towards the Pacific Ocean which was quite some distance away. I had a nightmarish vision of every river in Asia carrying a similar load. On my return to Australia I heard a former Prime Minister, Tony Abbott, asserting in one forum that climate change was actually 'good' and in another that fears for plastic pollution of the oceans 'exaggerated'. The outrage in my reaction to his sophistry and cant finds expression through this poem."
<u>Note from George</u>:
Clinton Richard Dawkins, FRS FRSL is an English ethologist, evolutionary biologist, and author. He is an emeritus fellow of New College, Oxford, and was the University of Oxford's Professor for Public Understanding of Science from 1995 until 2008. He is a militant atheist,

known for his vociferous, aggressive polemic against world religions, especially Christianity.

[80] George Watt writes, "I heard on radio the great English comedian and raconteur, Bill Bailey, recount his experience of saving an eagle-owl from the cooking pot while visiting a restaurant in China. The poem, 'Eagle-Owl in a Yunan Chophouse' is a speculative re-imagining of that event. While hopefully capturing the magic spirit of the bird's release into the wild, and the nobility of the creature itself, this poem does not claim historical verisimilitude in its telling. I should also stress that the poem is in no way critical of the eating habits of the Chinese. After all, animals eaten all over the world have as much right to life as this wonderful bird. The poem might well be an unwitting argument in support of vegetarianism and/or a reaffirmation of the inherent beauty in all living things."
<u>Notes from George</u>:
"gweilo": A Cantonese term for Caucasians. It can be either derogatory or affectionate, depending on the context.
 "Yangguizi": Putonghua for "foreign devil".

[81] Mocco Wollert's poem, 'Plastic' was inspired by a visit to the Sydney, Australia, Aquarium where Mocco saw a large display showing how one plastic bag can kill seven marine creatures.

[82] Mocco Wollert writes, "I am in awe of modern technology that creates 3D printed plastic limbs and organs which give people quality of life and their independence. However, I fear the misuse of this technology in the future."

[83] Maggie Wong writes this about her poem, 'The Declaration of Plastic': "I chose to write a poem about plastic, the selected topic of the year, since I considered it a huge challenge. Firstly, I only learned about the competition from one of my friends shortly before the deadline, which meant I had to get the task done without procrastination. Secondly, 'Plastic' is not an easy topic to be written about in

the form of poetry. Thirdly, I have written more than seven hundred poems all based on self-decided topics and themes instead of a specific one chosen by another party. Then I decided to make a serious attempt.

"Actually, it can easily fall into a clichéd or lecturing tone if the poem is written from the angle of a human about how plastic abuse has damaged the Earth and its ecosystem. So I imagined it from the point of view of plastic as an arrogant monster, narrating the problems, sufferings and crises caused by the overuse of the non-degradable material.

"It is very true that I am upset whenever I see pictures of how marine creatures are trapped by plastic packaging materials or killed after shallowing them. When I was writing the poem, images and pictures of the miserable sea creatures, and of gigantic mountains of plastic waste, kept recurring in my mind.

"My poem, written as plastic in the first person, starts with the compo of the material and when it was invented. Then comes the depiction of its continuous rampant growth due to people's indulgence in plastic simply for convenience. In the middle of the poem, a contrast between the earth before and after the ruins caused is made to illustrate what environmental damage has been caused by the abuse of plastic.

"The ending through the declaration of plastic as a warning to everyone, dissuading each individual from using the detrimental material, otherwise the consequences will be irreversibly disastrous."

[84] The world's first fully synthetic plastic was bakelite, invented in New York in 1907, by Leo Baekeland.— *Wikipedia*

[85] Marjorie Woodfield writes, "'She visits from New Zealand' was written when we were living in Saudi Arabia and took our daughter to the ancient Nabatean city of Madain Saleh. 'Al Hijir' means 'the place of stones', and the Arabic translates literally as, 'the archaeological

abandonment site of the city of Madain Saleh'. We explored the desert necropolis and marvelled at iconic stone-cut tombs with their distinctive façades and funerary motifs. We visited the oasis village of Al Ula, saw remnants of the Hejaz Railway and searched for desert diamonds. These small milky stones, also known as Qaisumah diamonds, can be cut and polished to an astonishing brilliance. My poem is strongly elegiac. The loss of a daughter whose visit is ending. The small village and ancient city, both empty and silent."

ADVANCE RESPONSES

Mingled Voices 4 anthologises a number of poems entered into a competition where the theme was 'Plastic'; a word which implies both the destructiveness of contemporary capitalist throw-away culture whose impact we are only just discovering, but which also implies the ability to mould, to shape. It was Coleridge in *Biographia Literaria* who created the word 'the esemplastic' out of the Greek to describe the power of the imagination: for Coleridge, the great Romantic poet, the imagination was the indispensable force for the creation of poetry, poetry being what comes out of nothing, like the Creation. The voices in this anthology describe experience, sometimes very fully; they are also aware of the power of poetry to shape experience (as in the winning piece, 'Waiting for Ulysses'), and of the power of music to shape eroticism, as in Ahmed Elbeshlawy's 'The Message of the Music', which comments ironically on the idealism which Coleridge's idea of the esemplastic power of the imagination presupposes. Many poems here struggle valiantly between the throw-away plastic, and the power of the imagination; but we may wonder too whether the individual imagination is enough to deal with the forces of detritus and disposability which affect nations and individual lives, and the lives of the planet alike.

—Jeremy Tambling, PhD
  teaches as Professor of English at SWAP University
  Warsaw, and used to be Professor of Comparative
  Literature in Hong Kong, and Professor of Literature at
  Manchester before retiring.

Mingled Voices 4 is an unusually powerful collection of works unfolding an engagement with space and time that is highly topical and arresting. In Maria Blanco's 'Waiting for Ulysses,' the speaker occupies many "places" in time and turns the space of a passive muse counterclockwise so that ironically, the patriarchal hero must locate a language where his Penelope feels his respect for her dignity if he is to rediscover the safe confines of home. 'A stranger on the street' by Aiden Huang meditates on whether home in the modern city is present or whether it has become submerged beneath the "gentrification" which has smoothed out the jagged lines composing a "dubious past". The speaker in the café feels the discordancy of modernity where a soft light amplifies his uneasiness and discord.

The suggested theme of the submissions, "plastic", invites the attention to the relation between a speaker and a modern space. In Vincent Casaregola's 'The Plastic Dead,' the speaker applies the trope of plastic to figure an unnaturally playful view of war. Carol Flake Chapman in 'Under the Blue Tarps' envisions a material that ironically shields us from the natural elements of 'wind' and 'rain.' Annie Christain gives in '"Appearances" from *Criminal Cipher Code for Police Officers*' a snapshot of plastic through the lens of a postmodern investigation. *Mingled Voices 4* is thusly a diverse collection, featuring poetry that is innovative and passionate in its engagement with significant challenges facing contemporary societies. It is well worth the read.

—Charles Lowe, PhD
Associate Dean / Associate Professor, Director of
English Language and Literature Studies Programme,
Division of Humanities and Social Sciences, United
International College (UIC), Zuhai, China.

SOME POETRY AND POETRY COLLECTIONS
Published by Proverse Hong Kong

Alphabet, by Andrew S. Guthrie. 2015.

Astra and Sebastian, by L.W. Illsley. 2011.

Bliss of Bewilderment, by Birgit Bunzel Linder. 2017.

The Burning Lake, by Jonathan Locke Hart. 2016.

Celestial Promise, by Hayley Ann Solomon. 2017.

Chasing light, by Patricia Glinton Meicholas. 2013.

China suite and other poems,
by Gillian Bickley. 2009.

Epochal Reckonings, by J.P. Linstroth. 2020. (Scheduled)

For the record and other poems of Hong Kong,
by Gillian Bickley. 2003.

Frida Kahlo's cry and other poems,
by Laura Solomon. 2015.

Heart to Heart: Poems, by Patty Ho. 2010.

Home, away, elsewhere,
by Vaughan Rapatahana. 2011.

Immortelle and bhandaaraa poems,
by Lelawattee Manoo-Rahming. 2011.

In vitro, by Laura Solomon. 2nd ed. 2014.

Irreverent poems for pretentious people,
by Henrik Hoeg. 2016.

The layers between (essays and poems),
by Celia Claase. 2015.

Of leaves & ashes, by Patty Ho. 2016.

Life Lines, by Shahilla Shariff. 2011.

*Mingled voices: the international Proverse Poetry Prize
anthology 2016,*
edited by Gillian and Verner Bickley. 2017.

*Mingled voices 2: the international Proverse Poetry Prize
anthology 2017,*
edited by Gillian and Verner Bickley. 2018.

*Mingled voices 3: the international Proverse Poetry Prize
anthology 2018,*
edited by Gillian and Verner Bickley. 2019.

Moving house and other poems from Hong Kong,
by Gillian Bickley. 2005.

Over the Years: Selected Collected Poems, 1972-2015,
by Gillian Bickley. 2017.

Painting the borrowed house: poems,
by Kate Rogers. 2008.

Perceptions, by Gillian Bickley. 2012.

Poems from the Wilderness, by Jack Mayer. 2020.
(Scheduled)

Rain on the pacific coast,
by Elbert Siu Ping Lee. 2013.

refrain, by Jason S. Polley. 2010.

Savage Charm, by Ahmed Elbeshlawy. 2019

Shadow play, by James Norcliffe. 2012.

Shadows in deferment, by Birgit Bunzel Linder. 2013.

Shifting sands, by Deepa Vanjani. 2016.

Sightings: a collection of poetry, with an essay, 'communicating poems', by Gillian Bickley. 2007.

Smoked pearl: poems of Hong Kong and beyond, by Akin Jeje (Akinsola Olufemi Jeje). 2010.

Of symbols misused, by Mary-Jane Newton. 2011.

The Hummingbird Sometimes Flies Backwards, by D.J. Hamilton. 2019.

The Year of the Apparitions, by José Manuel Sevilla. 2020 (Scheduled)

Unlocking, by Mary-Jane Newton. March 2014.

Violet, by Carolina Ilica. March 2019.

Wonder, lust & itchy feet, by Sally Dellow. 2011.

FIND OUT MORE ABOUT OUR AUTHORS, BOOKS, EVENTS AND LITERARY PRIZES

Visit our website: http://www.proversepublishing.com

Visit our distributor's website: www.cup.cuhk.edu.hk

Follow us on Twitter
Follow news and conversation: twitter.com/Proversebooks
OR
Copy and paste the following to your browser window and follow the instructions:
https://twitter.com/#!/ProverseBooks

"Like" us on www.facebook.com/ProversePress

Request our free E-Newsletter
Send your request to info@proversepublishing.com.

Availability
Available in Hong Kong and world-wide from our Hong Kong based distributor, The Chinese University of Hong Kong Press, The Chinese University of Hong Kong, Shatin, NT, Hong Kong SAR, China.
Email: cup@cuhk.edu.hk
Website: www.cup.cuhk.edu.hk.
All titles are available from Proverse Hong Kong, http://www.proversepublishing.com

Stock-holding retailers
Hong Kong (CUHKP, Bookazine)
Canada (Elizabeth Campbell Books),
Andorra (Llibreria La Puça, La Llibreria).

Orders may be made from bookshops in the UK and elsewhere.

Ebooks
Most of our titles are available also as Ebooks.